Real Girls of the Bible

Other Books in the Growing Faithgirlz!™ Library

The Faithgirlz! Bible

NIV Faithgirlz! Backpack Bible

Faithgirlz! Bible Study

The Secret Power of Modesty: The Book of 1 Peter

The Secret Power of Joy: The Book of Philippians

The Secret Power of Goodness: The Book of Colossians

The Secret Power of Love: The Book of Ruth

Nonfiction

Faithgirlz Journal

Faithgirlz Handbook

Faithgirlz! Cookbook

No Boys Allowed: Devotions for Girls

What's a Girl to Do? Finding Faith in Everyday Life

Girlz Rock: Devotions for You

Chick Chat: More Devotions for Girls

Faithgirlz! Whatever!

My Beautiful Daughter: What It Means to Be Loved by God

Beauty Lab

Body Talk

Everybody Tells Me to Be Myself, But I Don't Know Who I Am

Girl Politics

Fiction

Sophie Series

Sophie's World

Sophie's Secret

Sophie Under Pressure

Sophie Steps Up

Sophie's First Dance

Sophie's Stormy Summer

Sophie's Friendship Fiasco

Sophie and the New Girl

Sophie Flakes Out

Sophie Loves Jimmy

Sophie's Drama

Sophie Gets Real

Girls of Harbor View

Girl Power

Rescue Chelsea

Raising Faith

Secret Admirer

Check out www.faithgirlz.com

Real Girls
of the
Bible
A 31-Day Devotional

Written by Mona Hodgson

ZONDERVAN.com/
AUTHORTRACKER
follow your favorite authors

ZONDERKIDZ

Real Girls of the Bible
Copyright © 2008, 2011 by Mona Hodgson

This title is also available as a Zondervan ebook.
Visit www.zondervan.com/ebooks.

Requests for information should be addressed to:
Zonderkidz, *Grand Rapids, Michigan 49530*

978-0-310-73018-7

Published in association with the literary agency of Janet Kobobel Grant, Books
& Such, 52 Mission Circle, Suite 122, PMB 170, Santa Rosa, California 95409-5370,
www.booksandsuch.biz.

Zonderkidz is a trademark of Zondervan.

Art direction: Sarah Molegraaf
Cover design: Cindy Davis
Interior design: Christine Orejuela-Winkleman
Interior composition: Greg Johnson/Textbook Perfect

Printed in the United States of America

11 12 13 14 15 16 /DCI/ 20 19 18 17 16 15 14 13 12 11 10 9 8 7 6 5 4 3 2

To my mom, June Gansberg Jensen,
who brought Bible people to life
for me on a flannel board

♡

To Shirley Millar, my friend in sunshine and storms—
a real girl of the Bible

♡

To Bob Hodgson, my hubby of 40 years, who inspires
me to become a real girl of the Bible

♡

I'd like to thank the following people:

- Robin Crouch, a former editor at Zonderkidz, who birthed the vision for this book and entrusted me to run with it. Her cheers still ring in my ears.
- My agent, Janet Kobobel Grant, from Books & Such, Inc. for her years of partnership, patience, and toting pompoms. Thanks for cheering me onward.
- Barbara Scott and Betsy Flikkema, my former editors at Zonderkidz, for coming alongside me and taking this book to the finish line.
- My prayer partners—Shirley, June, Ann, and Karen—whose faithful prayers brought *Real Girls of the Bible* to life and gave it legs. And to all the others who listened to the Holy Spirit's prompting and breathed prayers for me and this book and the girls who will read it.
- My Snoopy Dancer writing buds—Lauraine, Eileen, Ceil, Diana, Nancy Jo, Paddy, and Kathleen—who celebrate the book's completion with me.
- My true inspiration for becoming a real girl of the Bible and writing about it—Jesus. It's all because of him.

Contents

PART TWO
New Testament Girls

Introduction

Hi there,
Do you have a favorite Bible girl? Esther has been one of my favorites for a long time. Beauty. Royalty. Intrigue. Bravery. Victory. What a story! But several other Bible girls have also captured my attention and tugged on my heart.

There's Leah's victorious story of sibling rivalry and her search for love and acceptance.

And Ruth. She left her home, family, and familiar traditions to travel to a strange land with her mother-in-law. A terrific story of friendship and faith.

On paper I've met Mary, Eve, Lydia, and many other fascinating Bible girls I want you to meet. Here you will read about thirty amazing girls of faith with guts *and* grace whose journeys give us glimpses of God. They show us who God is, how much he cares about you and me, and how much he longs for a real relationship with each one of us.

In this book, you'll get to know some of the Bible girls better and meet some you hadn't even heard of. They all inspire me to be a real girl of the Bible. I hope they do the same for you.

While getting to know our Bible girls, I also discovered extra tidbits about them and their culture that I thought you might enjoy too. So check it all out.

Happy reading, fellow *real* girl,

Mona

What Is a
Real Girl of the Bible?

A real girl is ... R E A L !

Relational

> To all who received [Jesus], to those who
> believed in his name, he gave the right to
> become children of God.
>
> —JOHN 1:12

Exalting

> You are my God, and I will give you thanks;
> you are my God, and I will exalt you.
>
> —PSALM 118:28

Authentic

> "The LORD does not look at the things man looks
> at. Man looks at the outward appearance, but
> the LORD looks at the heart."
>
> —1 SAMUEL 16:7

Loving

> Love the LORD your God with all your heart and with all your soul and with all your strength.
>
> —DEUTERONOMY 6:5

> Love each other as I have loved you.
>
> —JOHN 15:12

A real girl of the Bible enjoys a personal and purposeful relationship with God — one that influences her relationships with others. A real girl is developing a thankful heart, recognizing God's importance in her life, and exalting his name. A real girl is ... well, *real*, and confident in who she is because of Christ. A real girl desires to love her Lord with all her heart and with everything she has and is. And that love guides her love for all others.

PART 1

Old Testament Girls

Chapter 1

Eve's Too-Late Discovery

Read Eve's story in Genesis 2:15–4:1.

Psalm 139:13–14 says, "You knit me together in my mother's womb. I praise you because I am fearfully and wonderfully made." But it was different for Eve. God took a rib from Adam and made Eve, the first female on earth.

Right from the start God established that he had a special purpose for Eve. God formed Eve to be a friend, helper, and wife to the only other person on earth, Adam.

Talk about a great beginning! Eve lived in a garden full of flowering plants and tons of trees that produced yummy fruit. And Eve and Adam could pick fruit from any tree except the one in the middle of the garden. God had told them not to eat the fruit of that tree.

Red and blue and yellow birds flitted around the garden of Eden warbling songs of praise to the Creator. Animals of every kind roamed and romped all around Eve in her up-close and personal zoo. Adam and Eve enjoyed nature walks and long talks. All was well between Eve and God.

Until that day.

While Eve strolled the gorgeous garden, a serpent slithered out on a branch and spoke to her. "Did God really say you couldn't eat from every tree in the garden?"

"We may eat fruit from the trees," Eve said, "but God said not to eat fruit from the tree in the middle of the garden. He said if we touched it, we'd die."

"That's silly. You won't die," the serpent sneered. "God doesn't want you to eat it because when you do, your eyes will open and you'll be like him."

Eve stared at the smooth and shiny fruit on the tree in the middle of the garden. The fruit was so pretty to look at — ripe and ready to eat. Tempted, Eve picked the fruit and ate some. Then she gave it to her husband, Adam, who also bit into it.

Satan, the crafty con, had disguised himself as a serpent to tempt Eve. And his half-truth worked. He'd told Eve that when she ate of the fruit, her eyes would open. They did, and Eve saw that she and her husband were naked. According to Satan, Eve would be like God when she ate the fruit. She wasn't all-powerful like God, but she did learn the difference between good and evil. Because Eve felt guilty for disobeying God, she and Adam picked leaves from a fig tree and sewed them together.

Later when Adam and Eve heard the Lord strolling in the garden, they ducked behind a tree and hid from him.

Have you ever done something you knew was wrong and felt guilty about it? Have you ever tried to hide what you did from your parents or a teacher? Can you hide from God? Could Eve?

God knew what Eve and her husband had done and why they'd hidden from him. Because God loved them, he showed them grace and used animal skins to make better clothes for them. But Eve still suffered the consequences of her sin. No more strolls in the beautiful garden with God. She and her husband had to leave the garden, and life became hard. They had to work for their food. Her pain in having babies was increased, but God gave Eve the strength she needed.

If you were out milking the goats with Eve today, she'd probably warn you about your enemy Satan. She'd tell you Satan has an evil plan for everyone who knows and loves God. But she'd also tell you God has a good and perfect plan for your life.

Eve would tell you Satan had taken the form of a serpent and twisted what God had said into a lie. Because Eve didn't know about Satan's persuasive powers, she'd listened to him and reached for the forbidden fruit. She might wipe tears from her cheeks and tell you God is a good God. That he'll love you even when you mess up.

Eve had to live with the consequences of her disobedience, but God still provided for her needs.

The Bible says we've all sinned. We don't always do what's right. Like Eve, we're sometimes tempted to want things and relationships that aren't good for us.

Are you ever tempted to listen to the wrong people? Kids at school, friends in the neighborhood, or even a brother or sister can make bad things look pretty good to us.

When you're tempted, you can remember Eve's story. You can choose to listen to God and trust his love for you. When you do make a bad choice and mess up, you can go to God, confess your sin to him, and accept his gracious forgiveness.

From GOD'S Heart

Jesus said to [Satan], "Away from me, Satan! For it is written: 'Worship the Lord your God, and serve him only.'"

—Matthew 4:10

I will turn away from Satan and his sneaky ways and follow God's holy ways.

Dear God ...

Father God, help me to recognize temptation for what it is and help me to refuse to go against you and your Word. In Jesus's name, amen.

$\mathcal{E}$ve was the first woman and a woman of firsts. She was

Check THIS Out

> the first woman to walk
>   with God,
> the first wife,
> the first person to disobey God and sin,
> the first woman to receive God's grace,
> the first woman to sew a piece of clothing,
> the first woman to give birth to a child, and
> the first mother to lose a child.

Mary the mother of Jesus came through Eve's third son, Seth, whose name means *compensation*, which is "payment." Jesus was the perfect one who could pay for our sins.

Chapter 2

Sarah's Big Surprise

Read Sarah's story in Genesis 12:1–15;
16:1–6; 17:1–8, 15–17; 18:1–15; 21:1–7.

Sarai, later called Sarah, was a princess. Her name even meant "princess." But Sarai's castle was a tent pitched here and there from Mesopotamia to Haran to the land of Canaan.

Sarai was married to Abram, a man ten years older than her. The Lord had told Abram to leave his people and his country of Mesopotamia and take off for a land God would later show him. So at sixty-five years old, Sarai packed up and headed out on an adventure with her husband and his nephew Lot.

Sarai knew the Lord had promised Abram he'd be the father of a great nation and many generations would come from him. She also knew in order for God to make a great nation from their children, she'd have to have babies who would grow up and have babies. But their cradle was empty. And in that day if a woman couldn't have children, people thought God had cursed her. That she'd done something to make God mad at her.

Ten years had passed since God's promise to give Sarai and Abram children. She was seventy-five years old. She wasn't getting any younger, and she still hadn't had a baby. So she decided that if her maid had a baby with Abram, it would fulfill God's promise.

Sarai went to Abram and said, "The Lord won't give me children. Go sleep with my maidservant so I can build a family through her." Then Sarai gave her Egyptian maidservant, Hagar, to Abram. Sarai's plan turned out to be a painful one. When Hagar became pregnant, she began to hate Sarai.

Sarai blamed Abram. "You're responsible for my suffering," she told him. "Now that Hagar knows she's pregnant, she hates me."

"She's your servant," Abram said. "You should do whatever you think is best."

Hagar had given Abram something Sarai hadn't been able to give him: a child. And having Hagar around reminded Sarai she didn't have a child of her own. She became jealous of Hagar and made her life miserable, so Hagar ran away.

But God still had his own plan. The Lord came to Abram again. While Abram was facedown on the ground before him, God promised Abram again that he'd be the father of many nations. God changed Abram's name to Abraham and Sarai's name to Sarah.

"I'll bless Sarah and give you a son by her," God said, "She'll be the mother of nations. Kings will come from her."

Sarah laughed at the thought that she, a ninety-year-old woman, could be having a baby. But nothing gets in the way of God's plan. When Sarah gave birth to a son, they named him Isaac. The name *Isaac* means "laughter." Sarah said, "God has brought me laughter, and everyone who hears about this will laugh with me. Who would've thought I'd nurse a child at my age?"

God knew it would happen. But before Princess Sarah learned to wait for God, she was a royal pain. Sarah's impatience to have a baby, her moments of doubting God's promises, and her poor choices in trying to make it happen with Hagar caused Sarah and others a lot of trouble.

Sarah learned that God uses a different clock than we do. God keeps his promises, but he does it in his perfect time. And God's perfect time for something to happen isn't usually soon enough for us.

Sarah's son, Isaac, did become the father of the nation of Israel. It just didn't happen as soon as she wanted it to.

Have you ever prayed and prayed and waited and waited for something? Have you ever lost your patience with God? Maybe you prayed for a new brother or sister. Or you asked God to help you pass a math test you studied for. Maybe you prayed for your parents to get back together. Sometimes God says no. Sometimes he says yes. Other times he'll tell you to wait. Waiting is hard. But God always knows what's best.

From GOD'S Heart

"My thoughts are not your thoughts, neither are your ways my ways," declares the LORD. "As the heavens are higher than the earth, so are my ways higher than your ways and my thoughts than your thoughts."

—Isaiah 55:8–9

I will trust God's higher thoughts and ways and wait for his perfect plan for me.

Dear God . . .

Lord, please help me remember that your way is best. Help me wait for you with patience and peace. Amen.

For many people in Bible times, camping wasn't just something they did on weekends or on vacations. It was their way of life.

Check THIS Out

Today some of the Bedouin people still live in similar tents in the deserts of the Middle East.

Sarah became known and respected as the mother of Israel, not because of what she did, but because of God's divine plan, and because he kept his promise to Abraham.

Chapter 3

Hagar's Desert
Revelation

Read Hagar's story in Genesis 16; 21:8–21.

When a famine hit Canaan, Abram and Sarai traveled to Egypt. Genesis 12:10–20 tells the story. Sarai was a beautiful woman. Abram feared that when the Egyptian men saw Sarai, they'd kill him so they could have her. Abram told Sarai to tell them she was his sister so they'd spare his life and treat them well.

Sarai was taken to Pharaoh's palace. And because of Sarai, Pharaoh treated Abram well. He gave Abram sheep, cattle, donkeys, camels, and servants. That's probably when Hagar stepped into the family picture. She was an Egyptian girl who became a maidservant to Sarai. Slavery is no longer legal, but at that time, slavery was acceptable and common.

Because Hagar was Sarai's servant, when Sarai decided Hagar could have a baby for her, Hagar didn't have much say in the matter. The Bible doesn't tell us what Hagar's feelings were at that point, but it does say that after Hagar became pregnant, she began to hate Sarai.

Not a good thing. Hagar became proud that she could have Abram's child and Sarai couldn't. But Hagar's bad attitude caught up with her. Sarai mistreated her. Pregnant and alone, Hagar ran away from Abram and Sarai's home.

An angel of the Lord found Hagar near a spring in the desert. "Hagar, servant of Sarai," he said, "where have you come from and where are you going?"

"I'm running away from Sarai," Hagar said.

"Go back and obey her," the angel of the Lord said. "I'll increase your offspring. There will be too many to count. You'll have a son. Name him Ishmael, for the Lord has heard of your suffering."

Then Hagar said, "You're the God who sees me. Now I've seen the one who sees me."

Hagar returned to Abram and Sarai's home and had a son. She named him Ishmael, just as the Lord had said.

Fourteen years later, Sarai, whose name had been changed to Sarah, gave birth to Isaac. Ishmael was a teenager and Isaac a toddler when Ishmael teased Isaac. Sarah became angry and again wanted Hagar and Ishmael to leave her home.

God told Abram, now known as Abraham, to let Hagar and Ishmael go as part of God's plan. Early the next morning, Abraham gave Hagar food, an animal-skin canteen full of water, and then sent them back into the desert. When the water ran out, Hagar left her son under a bush, sat nearby, and cried.

God called to Hagar from heaven. "What's the matter, Hagar? Don't be afraid. God hears the boy crying. Lift the boy and take his hand. I'll make him into a great nation."

Hagar and Ishmael were out in the middle of nowhere, and God heard their cries, just as he hears your cries and sees your tears today.

When God opened Hagar's eyes, she saw a well of water. She filled the skin with water and gave Ishmael a drink.

God was with the boy as he grew. God kept his promise to Hagar too. Ishmael became the father of a great nation. His twelve sons became the rulers of twelve tribes—a people called the Ishmaelites.

The first time the Lord spoke to Hagar in the desert, he told her to go back home to Sarai. The next time she was in the desert, she and her son were near death. But God came to her and provided a well of water for them to drink. God took care of them.

As God said to Hagar, he says to you, "Don't be afraid. I hear your cries. I see your troubles. And though life will be hard sometimes, I am with you and I will take care of you."

From GOD'S Heart

O Lord, you have searched me and you know me. You know when I sit and when I rise; you perceive my thoughts from afar.

—Psalm 139:1–2

I will remember that God is always
with me, and I can always talk to him
about my life.

Dear God . . .

Dear heavenly father, thank you for knowing
me and loving me. Thank you for being a friend
who is always with me. Amen.

Check THIS Out

Giving God a new name was unusual in the Old Testament, but Hagar did it when she called God, "the God who sees me."

Mount Sinai is the place where God gave Moses the Ten Commandments. Did you know that the Arabic name for Mount Sinai is Mount Hagar?

The Egyptian name *Pharaoh* isn't a personal name. It's a royal title that means "great house." Pharaohs lived in fancy palaces.

Real-Girl *Desert* Tips

Since many of our Bible girls spent a lot of time in the desert, if they were here, they'd probably give you some desert tips.

1. Wear shoes when you go outside to protect your feet from rough rocks, plant spines, and crawly critters.
2. Carry water with you and drink plenty of it to guard against dehydration in the dry desert climate.
3. Wear sunscreen to protect your skin from over-exposure to the sun.
4. Always have a walking or hiking partner with you so that if you have any problems, you have someone with you to help you or to go for help.
5. Only walk on trails so that you have a clear view of your immediate surroundings. That will help protect you from spiny plants and surprises like snakes and coyotes.
6. Stay alert while hiking or camping so that you're aware of the presence of other people and any desert critters.

7. Keep your hands and feet where you can see them. You don't want to be surprised by any critters that might want to sting or bite you.

8. When you hike, wear heavy shoes or boots to protect your feet from rocks, scorpions, and snakes.

9. Shake out clothing, shoes, towels, blankets, and other things that have been left outside to make sure no desert critters have nested in them.

10. Give insects and animals plenty of room to get away from you.

Chapter 4

Leah's
Rival

Read Leah's story in Genesis 29:4–35; 30:17–24;
31:3–7; 33:1–7; 35:16–19; 49:29–31.

All her life Leah lived in the shadow of her younger sister, Rachel. Rachel was pretty. Leah was plain and had weak eyes. Because they didn't have glasses then, Leah probably bumped into things. Life was tough for Leah. She also had a father, Laban, who was a selfish and tricky man.

Leah and Rachel's cousin, Jacob, showed up at Laban's well one day. Rachel was bringing her flock of sheep to the well when Jacob saw her. She was so beautiful he probably stared at her. While Rachel ran and told her father their relative had arrived, Jacob watered his uncle's sheep.

After Jacob had stayed with Laban, Rachel, and Leah for a month, Laban said, "Just because you're a relative, that doesn't mean you should work for nothing. What do you want to get paid?"

Jacob was in love with Rachel, so he said, "I'll work for you for seven years in return for your younger daughter, Rachel." In that place and time, it wasn't illegal for cousins to marry one another like it is today in America. Laban agreed to the deal.

After seven years, Laban hosted a big wedding feast. When the evening came, he gave his daughter in marriage to Jacob.

When the sun rose the next morning, Jacob saw he was with Leah, not with Rachel, the woman he loved. "What have you done to me?" Jacob asked Laban, "I served you so I could marry Rachel. Why have you tricked me?"

Laban said, "It's not our custom to give the younger daughter in marriage before the older one. I'll also let you marry my younger daughter in return for another seven years of work." So Jacob finally married Rachel.

The Bible says Jacob loved Rachel more than Leah. Leah had been forced to marry a man who didn't want her. And he'd pushed her aside for her pretty little sister. Leah must've felt inferior, unwanted, and jealous.

The two sisters competed for Jacob's attention and affection. Rachel wasn't able to give Jacob children for many years. But God gave Leah many sons. Every time Leah gave birth to a son, she thought maybe then Jacob would love her.

Leah named her fourth son Judah, which means "praised." Leah had surrendered to God's plan, and she said, "This time I will praise the Lord." She'd been trying to earn Jacob's affection. Leah learned it's more important to know God loves you and cares about you than it is to make sure everybody else loves you. We don't have control over how people feel about us. Leah had been manipulated by her father and upstaged by her sister. She struggled with jealousy. But Leah didn't choose bitterness. Instead she was thankful for her children. With each son God gave Leah, she grew in inner beauty.

Leah, not Rachel, was destined to be Jacob's first and last wife. Leah outlived Rachel. And in the end, Jacob chose to be buried with Leah, not with Rachel. Did Jacob finally realize how badly he'd treated Leah? Did he finally see that Leah loved him and served him even though he didn't deserve it? Maybe.

Like Leah, you may compete with someone in your life. Maybe it's a sibling, cousin, or friend. Do you compare yourself with other girls, TV stars, or magazine models? Do you judge other people by what they look like on the outside? Do you decide to like someone or not because of what they wear?

God loves you because you're you. He sees and knows your heart and soul. Does he see Jesus in your life?

From GOD'S Heart

The Lord does not look at the things man looks at. Man looks at the outward appearance, but the Lord looks at the heart.

—1 Samuel 16:7

I will keep my heart focused on God and
try to see people as God sees them.

Dear God . . .

Lord God, I'm so glad you love me for who I
am. That's what matters most. Help me to not
compare myself to the people around me, on
TV, or in magazines. For Jesus's sake, amen.

Jacob had twelve sons (from oldest to youngest) — Reuben, Simeon, Levi, Judah, Dan, Issachar, Gad, Asher, Naphtali, Zebulun, Joseph, and Benjamin. Ten of the twelve tribes of Judah were named after Jacob's sons. Levi and Joseph did not have tribes named after them. Instead, the remaining two tribes were named after Joseph's sons.

Check THIS Out

In Bible times, the bride and groom usually didn't choose one another. Their parents decided who would marry their son or daughter and arranged the marriage.

Chapter 5

A Royal Gift for Jochebed

Read Jochebed's story in Exodus 1:15–22; 2:1–10.

*P*icture this: You're a Hebrew girl. You and your people are slaves in Egypt, which is a foreign land. You get married and begin a family. You have a daughter and two sons. One of your sons isn't even old enough to roll over yet. Your newborn coos, drools, and still nurses at your breast.

Now imagine that the pharaoh in Egypt orders that all Hebrew baby boys be killed. He doesn't want any more Israelites around who could grow up and fight him. Pharaoh tells the midwives, "When you help the Hebrew women in childbirth, if the baby is a boy, kill him." Because the midwives didn't kill the baby boys, Pharaoh told his people to throw the boys born to Hebrew women into the Nile.

The tiny bundle in your quivering arms—your son—is a Hebrew baby boy.

That picture was real life for Jochebed.

The Hebrew midwives didn't turn in Jochebed when they helped her have her baby. Jochebed's daughter, Miriam, and son Aaron both kept quiet about their new baby brother. But the baby was growing and making more noise. Jochebed wouldn't be able to hide him from Pharaoh and his people much longer. And when they found the baby boy, they'd drown him in the Nile. If he wasn't discovered and he did live, he would grow up as a slave.

Jochebed could've given up, but she didn't. She knew the stories about God's faithfulness to Abraham and Sarah. And she trusted God with her son's life.

Jochebed wove a basket out of papyrus and then coated it with tar and pitch to waterproof it. She kissed her baby boy's soft cheek, tucked him into the basket, and clutched it as she walked. Praying, Jochebed asked God to protect her son's life. And then she set the basket in the reeds along the bank of the Nile River and told her daughter Miriam to watch.

What would happen to him? Jochebed's walk home must have been tough. Her son couldn't feed himself. He couldn't change his own dirty diapers. He couldn't protect himself. And now the only chance Jochebed had of protecting her baby boy was to leave him alone.

Would God provide a way for her son to live?

At home while Jochebed cooked over the fire, she continued to pray for her baby. Then she heard Miriam's shouts.

"Mama, Mama, hurry. Come quick."

Oh no! Had something happened to her baby boy?

Jochebed hurried back to the place where she'd set the basket in the reeds. Nearby, she saw the pharaoh's daughter holding the baby.

Do you know what happened next?

Pharaoh's daughter paid Jochebed to take the baby home and nurse him until he was old enough to live in the palace. Pharaoh's daughter named the baby Moses and raised him safely as her son. God saved Moses from certain death. And he provided a way for Jochebed to be close to her son and care for him until he was older.

Behind the scenes, God worked out his plan for Jochebed, Moses, Aaron, and Miriam. God does the same thing for you. You may not always see God or hear him or even feel him at work in your life, but God is there. And like Jochebed, you can trust God to work through your circumstances for his purposes, which are always best.

From GOD'S Heart

I have learned to be content whatever the circumstances.

—Philippians 4:11

I will trust God with my circumstances —
the good ones and the bad ones.

God used women to keep the pharaoh from destroying the Israelites. He used the midwives, Jochebed, Miriam, and even the pharaoh's own daughter to save Moses, who would one day lead his people — the Israelites — out of captivity in Egypt.

Check THIS Out

Papyrus is a reed that grew near the River Nile. Papyrus was also used to make boats, ropes, sandals, and other things. Miriam's mother made a papyrus basket to lay baby Moses in.

The paper on which the ancient Word of God was written was also made from papyrus. The tall stems were cut thin and hammered together. The sheets were pasted end-to-end to form a roll called a scroll.

Chapter 6

Miriam's Journey

Read Miriam's story in Exodus 2:1–8; 14:5–15:21.

Miriam helped to save her brother from the cruel Egyptian pharaoh. Miriam watched as her mother bundled the three-month-old baby in a basket and hid the basket in the reeds along the bank of the River Nile. Miriam stayed by the basket to watch over her brother. Miriam was a Hebrew living as a slave—along with the other Israelites—under the rule of the Egyptian pharaoh. The pharaoh had demanded that all the Hebrew baby boys be killed as soon as they were born. Her mother had kept Miriam's baby brother safe until now, but his cries grew stronger. Soon Pharaoh's people would find him.

When Pharaoh's daughter strolled to the riverbank to bathe, she saw the basket and sent her slave to fetch it out of the water. Miriam's brother cried. Miriam hid and watched her brother intently. What would happen to him? Was there anything Miriam could do to save him?

"This is one of the Hebrew babies," Pharaoh's daughter said. "I want to keep it."

Miriam believed in God. She prayed and asked God for wisdom. Then Miriam stepped boldly out of the reeds and said to the pharaoh's daughter, "Do you want me to get one of the Hebrew women to nurse the baby for you?"

Pharaoh's daughter said, "Yes, go."

If you just read about Jochebed, Miriam's mother, you know that Pharaoh's daughter paid Miriam's mother to take baby Moses home and care for him until he was old enough to live in the palace. Because Miriam spoke up, with God's help, she was able to save her baby brother.

Years later, after ten terrible plagues, Pharaoh allowed Moses and Aaron to lead the Israelites out of Egypt to the land God had promised them. But before they got very far, Pharaoh changed his mind. He wanted the Israelites back in slavery. His army chased Moses, Miriam, and their people to the Red Sea.

Would they all be taken back to Egypt?

Just when the Israelites reached the water's edge, something amazing happened. God separated the waters and Miriam, Moses, and the Israelites crossed the sea on dry land.

But Pharaoh's army followed them. Would the Israelites ever get away from him and be free?

When all the Israelites were safe on the other side of the Red Sea, God let the water go. The waves rolled in on Pharaoh's men. But Moses, Aaron, Miriam, and their people were safe.

Because Miriam followed God's guidance when Moses was a baby, Moses survived to lead his people out of slavery. Even though our actions—like Miriam's—may seem small to us now, they can have big consequences in the future.

Do you know what Miriam did next? She became a worship leader. Miriam praised God with her tambourine. And all the women followed her, playing instruments and dancing for God while Miriam sang a chorus:

> "Sing to the LORD,
> for he is highly exalted.
> The horse and its rider
> he has hurled into the sea."

As a young girl, Miriam learned that God is faithful and just. She learned to trust God and to praise him. God is faithful to you too. Like Miriam, you can pay attention to God's work in your life and worship him. Think about all the times he's helped you, taken care of you, and blessed you. You can show your friends and family and the other people in your life how to be thankful and praise God.

From GOD'S Heart

Rejoice in the Lord always. I will say it again: Rejoice!

—Philippians 4:4

I will remember God's faithfulness
to me and praise him today.

Dear God . . .

Dear heavenly father, you are so good to me. Thank you for your goodness, Lord. Please help me to develop a thankful heart. I want to praise you more. For Jesus's sake, amen.

*L*ike you and me, Miriam was on a journey of faith. Sometimes she did things right. And sometimes she messed up and made mistakes. In Numbers 12:1–15, you can read about one of Miriam's bad choices, about the troubles it caused, and about God's great mercy.

Check THIS *Out*

Real-Girl *Skin Care* Tips

Miriam and many of the other Bible girls spent lots of time outside. If they were here today getting ready to hike or work in the garden with you, they'd probably have something to say about taking care of your skin when you're in the sun.

1. Too much exposure to the sun can cause skin spots, early wrinkles, and even skin cancer.
2. Dermatologists recommend using a sunscreen with an SPF (sun protection factor) of 15 or

higher. If you have light skin, you may need to use 30 or even 45 SPF.

3. Choose a sunscreen that'll protect your skin from both UVA and UVB rays, which are two different kinds of ultraviolet rays.

4. Apply sunscreen on all of your bare skin, not just your face.

5. Miriam likely wore a square of material on her head to protect her from the sun's heat. She'd probably tell you to wear a hat.

6. Even if you're under cloud coverage, you still need to wear sunscreen.

7. After you've splashed around in the water, reapply sunscreen.

Chapter 7

Rahab's Rooftop Hideaway

Read Rahab's story in Joshua 2:1–21; 6:1–25.

Rahab ran a business in Jericho. She welcomed travelers and entertained locals. Rahab's house sat right at the wall that surrounded the popular city of Jericho in the land of Canaan.

Instead of worshiping the one true God, Canaanites worshiped idols and false gods. Rahab was born and raised a Canaanite, but she'd heard the stories about how the pharaoh and his men chased the Israelites across the wilderness. She'd heard about God parting the Red Sea so the Israelites could cross it.

Rahab had also heard about the Hebrew people camped under the acacia trees east of the Jordan River, near her city. The city of Jericho was located at the entrance to the land God had promised the Israelites.

One day two Israelite spies showed up at Rahab's house. Joshua, the leader of the Israelites, had sent the men to check things out. The Bible doesn't say when or how Rahab learned the two men were spies, but she did find out and so did other people, including the king.

Rahab had a choice to make. Would she choose to turn the spies over to the king and become a hero in his eyes? Or would she keep the men safe?

Rahab chose to protect God's people. Choosing to believe in God, Rahab hid the two spies under the stalks of flax, a kind of grain, she had drying on her roof.

When the king's messengers told her to turn over the spies to them, she said, "The men came to me, but at dusk when it was time to close the city gate, the men left. Go quickly to catch up with them."

When the king's men hurried off, Rahab rushed up to the roof and said to the spies, "I know the Lord has given you this land. The Lord your God is God in heaven above and on the earth below. Show kindness to my family because I have shown kindness to you."

"Our lives for your lives," the spies said. "We'll treat you kindly."

Rahab let the two spies down by a rope through a window on the city wall. "Go to the hills," she told them. "Hide yourselves there three days and then go on your way."

The spies told Rahab she would be safe if she tied a scarlet cord in the window where she'd let them down. They also told her to make sure her father and mother, her brothers, and all her family were inside her house when the Israelites attacked.

When the spies left, Rahab tied the scarlet cord, her symbol of faith, in the window.

Later, as Joshua's army approached, the city was afraid and sealed itself shut. No one went out, and no one came in.

For six days, armed Israelite men and priests carrying trumpets marched around the outside of the city. On the seventh day, they marched around the city seven times and the priests blew horns. Then the Israelites shouted, and the wall around Jericho tumbled.

The Israelites took over the city. But because Rahab had turned away from the Canaanite idols and humbly placed her faith in God, Joshua and his army didn't harm Rahab or her family. Although Rahab had to see her city and people destroyed, God gave her an opportunity to know him and become a part of his chosen people. Rahab lived among the Israelites and eventually married a Jew named Salmon.

If Rahab could chat with you now, she'd probably tell you life is an adventure, and that every adventure requires faith in God. The courage to take risks comes from trusting God and knowing he's in the adventure with you.

From GOD'S Heart

As the body without the spirit is dead, so faith without deeds is dead.

—James 2:26

I will put my faith in God, and when action is required, I'll take action.

The scarlet cord the spies told Rahab to hang in her window was a red marker—red like the blood the Israelites placed over their doors on Passover (Exodus 12:13, 22–23). Both were a symbol of Christ's blood that he hadn't yet shed on the cross for our sins.

Check THIS Out

The trumpets the priests blew were made from rams' horns. They weren't made to be musical instruments. They were made to signal the Lord's plan to take over the city.

Jericho may be the world's oldest city. Records show it may have been built nearly 6,000 years before Miriam stopped wandering in the desert with the Israelites. Jericho's ancient ruins are located about seventeen miles northeast of Jerusalem.

Chapter 8

Deborah, Leader of a Nation

Read Deborah's story in Judges 4:1–17; 5:1–31.

Women in the ancient world didn't normally become political leaders, but Deborah was God's choice to serve as judge over Israel. At that time a judge was like a king.

Two hundred years had passed since Rahab had helped the spies escape Jericho, since Joshua and his men marched around the walls of Jericho, and since the walls crumbled. The Canaanites' King Jabin now dominated the Israelites. The Israelites had fallen from God again and worshiped the Canaanites' false gods and idols.

As God's leader of the Israelites, Deborah held court under a palm tree called the Palm of Deborah between Ramah and Bethel in the hill country of Ephraim. Listening to her people, she judged fairly and settled their arguments. Deborah's relationship with God shaped her worldview — the way she looked at the circumstances in the world. God knew she listened to his voice so he called her to deliver his people from the Canaanites.

When God told Deborah his plan, she sent for Barak, one of her military leaders, and gave him God's battle plan. "Take ten thousand men and lead them to Mount Tabor. God will lure Sisera, the commander of Jabin's army, to the Kishon River and give him into your hands."

Barak said, "I'll go, if you'll go with me."

Deborah must have had quite a reputation as a strong military leader and warrior since Barak would only go to battle if she went with him.

Deborah agreed to go with Barak and his army, but because he insisted she go with him, she said he wouldn't receive the honor for the victory. The honor would go to a woman. That was God's choice, and he used Deborah, the prophetess and judge, to announce it.

When Sisera heard that Barak and his army had gone up to Mount Tabor, he gathered his men and his nine hundred iron chariots in the Valley of Jezreel, along the Kishon River.

Deborah gave Barak the order to go, saying, "This is the day the Lord has given Sisera into your hands." Barak and his ten thousand men charged down Mount Tabor. Sisera's men had nine hundred chariots. Barak's men had none.

God sent a storm and flooded the area. Sisera left his chariot and took off on foot. Barak's army chased Sisera's chariots and army. All of Sisera's troops died.

Sisera ran like a coward. But just as Deborah had prophesied, God used a woman to hand Sisera over to Barak. (More details about that in Jael's chapter.)

On that day, the day of victory, Deborah and Barak sang a song of praise to God and thanks to the warriors who fought against the enemies of the Lord.

God requires a willing believer with a servant's heart to listen and lead according to his will. He used a humble and wise woman — Deborah — to direct the battle.

Are you a follower or a leader? If you're a follower, are you following the right person? Do you ever feel as if there's no godly person in your life to follow? Maybe your friends aren't the kind of leaders you should let lead you.

Are you a leader? Are you leading the people who follow you in the right direction? Are you leading them toward God or away from God?

Like Deborah, you can be a leader who loves God, listens to him, and leads others in his ways.

From GOD'S Heart

If any of you lacks wisdom, he should ask God, who gives generously to all without finding fault, and it will be given to him.

—James 1:5

I will seek God's wisdom so
I can serve him well.

Check THIS Out

There were six major judges in Israel's history: Othniel, Ehud, Deborah, Gideon, Jephthah, and Samson; and six minor judges: Shamgar, Tola, Jair, Ibzan, Elon, and Abdon. Deborah was the only female judge over Israel.

The name *Deborah* means "bee." That description fits this Deborah well. As a wife, leader of Israel, judge who settled arguments, and a prophetess who delivered God's truth, Deborah must have felt like a bee buzzing from one person and one place to another.

During Deborah's time, it was common practice to celebrate a national victory with songs. Deborah's song in Judges 5:2–31 is an early example of Hebrew poetry.

Chapter 9

Jael's Big Win

Read Jael's story in Judges 4:17–24.

From behind a flap of tent cloth, Jael watched the gathering clouds. Rain pounded the goat-skin covering that formed her house. She and her husband, Heber, were Kenites, a nomadic (traveling) tribe who lived in tents.

Heber had descended from Moses's brother-in-law, but he wasn't loyal to his Jewish heritage. Because Jael's husband didn't want trouble from the Canaanites, he accepted their evil ways and did nothing to stop them. According to Heber, his survival depended upon not taking sides with one group or the other.

Jael had heard rumors of wars. She knew the Canaanites had abused the Israelites.

Then one day a man on foot walked toward her tent. He was Sisera, the commander of King Jabin's

Canaanite army. Jael hurried out to meet him. Sisera had run away from the battle, and now he — the enemy of God and Jael's people — stood right in front of her. "Come, my lord," she said, "come right into my tent. Don't be afraid."

Then, though it was against their custom for a man to enter the tent of a woman who wasn't his wife, Sisera followed her inside. He probably thought it'd be the perfect hiding place.

"I'm thirsty," he said. "Please give me some water."

Jael opened a skin of milk — probably goat's milk — and gave Sisera a drink. When Sisera lay down, Jael covered him up. Once he fell asleep, Jael picked up a tent peg and a hammer. She tiptoed to the mat where Sisera lay. Then she drove the peg through his temple, killing him and defeating Israel's enemy. Jael's heart was with Israel. With God.

Soon Barak came searching for Sisera. Jael walked out to meet Barak, the Israelite commander. "Come," she said, "I'll show you the man you're looking for."

Barak followed Jael into her tent, where Sisera lay dead. A woman had the victory over Sisera, just as Deborah had prophesied to Barak.

On that day, God defeated King Jabin and ended his power over the Israelites.

When Jael saw Sisera at her tent, she saw her opportunity to end his abuse of Israel. And she took action.

In Judges 5:24, in Deborah's poem of victory, she said, "Most blessed of women be Jael, most blessed of tent-dwelling women."

When God's enemy showed up outside Jael's tent, she had a choice to make. Would she protect the evil Sisera, or would she do what God intended for her to do? She chose not to play it safe, and she did the right thing.

What about you? When you have to make a decision between right and wrong, do you do what seems easiest? Do you choose being popular over standing up to a challenge and doing what's right?

When you're tempted to do what someone else wants you to do even if it's wrong, ask God to give you the strength to stand for what is good and right.

From GOD'S Heart

Be strong in the Lord and in his mighty power.

—Ephesians 6:10

I will place my trust in the Lord and
be strong in his power.

Dear God ...

Lord God, I want to stand strong for you. Help me to trust you and then do the right thing in your strength. I love you, Lord. In Jesus's name, amen.

The people used the skins of goats or lambs to make containers for liquid, including milk.

Real-Girl *Spiritual Armor* Tips

Ephesians 6:10–18 talks about the kind of armor we should wear to protect ourselves against the "powers of this dark world and against the spiritual forces of evil." Satan is our true enemy. And as he did with Eve in the garden, Satan, or the Devil, knows how to use our hearts and minds to convince us to think and feel and act for his evil purposes.

Stand firm and put on your spiritual armor:

The belt of truth buckled around your waist—God is truth, and his kingdom is built on truth. You can stand on the truth of who God is and who you are because you have placed your trust in him.

The breastplate of righteousness in place—Righteousness is acting in agreement with God's law and following Jesus' example. Make choices that show you are strong with God's grace and love.

Feet fitted with the readiness that comes from the gospel of peace—As good shoes provide you with support on different surfaces, the gospel of peace also readies and supports you as you face different issues.

The shield of faith—Faith is putting your trust in God. Trusting him helps you resist temptations.

The helmet of salvation—Because of your faith in Jesus Christ, you are God's child and no one can take that away from you. Satan will aim his attacks at your mind with smooth talk, flattery, and trickery. Wear your helmet of faith to protect yourself with God's divine strength.

The sword of the Spirit—The sword of the Spirit is the powerful Word of God. Reading, memorizing, and praying Scripture will help you recognize and spoil Satan's attempts to discourage and defeat you.

The various pieces of the armor—truth, righteousness, readiness, faith, and a relationship with God are all cinched together in prayer. These pieces of the armor represent your spiritual growth and character development in Christ. And the more like Christ you become, the stronger you stand in spiritual battles.

Chapter 10

Naomi's Journey Home

Read Naomi's story in Ruth 1; 2:1–3; 2:20–3:4; 4:13–17.

Naomi and her husband, Elimelech, were Israelites born and raised in the Promised Land. When a famine hit and there wasn't enough food for everyone, Naomi, her husband, and their two boys moved from Bethlehem to Moab. In Bethlehem, Naomi's people worshiped God. Moabites, the people of Moab, worshiped false gods and idols.

Later, Elimelech died and left Naomi with two sons to care for. Her sons, Mahlon and Kilion, grew up and married Moabite women. And then after ten years of living in Moab, both of Naomi's sons died.

Naomi had lost everything that was important to her. She was a foreigner in Moab, and two daughters-in-law were all she had left. Naomi was homesick. The famine had ended in Israel so she decided to return to her birthplace of

Bethlehem in the land of Judah. Naomi and her daughters-in-law, Ruth and Orpah, packed their stuff.

Traveling gave Naomi lots of time to think. Ruth and Orpah had both been born and raised in Moab. And now she was leading her daughters-in-law away from their home. How could she ask them to leave their home, their families, and their way of life? How could she expect them to follow an old woman to a strange place and a foreign culture?

Naomi drew in a deep breath. "Go back," she said. "Both of you go back to your mother's home. May the Lord show kindness to you, as you have to my dead sons and to me." She kissed Ruth and Orpah goodbye. They wept and said, "We'll go with you to your people."

"Go home, my daughters," Naomi said. "Why would you come with me? Am I going to have any more sons who could become your husbands? No. The Lord's hand has moved against me." Although she loved her daughters-in-law, Naomi had nothing to offer Ruth and Orpah. She blessed them and prayed that they would find new rest and possibly new husbands in their own land—a better life than she could offer them.

Ruth and Orpah wept again. Then Orpah kissed her mother-in-law goodbye. But Ruth clung to Naomi. "Look," said Naomi, "your sister-in-law is going home to her people and her gods. Go with her."

With tears in her eyes, Ruth looked at Naomi and said, "Where you go I will go, and where you stay I will stay. Your people will be my people and your God my God."

That said, Ruth followed Naomi to Bethlehem. As Naomi and Ruth arrived, the women in Bethlehem hurried toward them. "Naomi, is it really you?

"Don't call me Naomi," she told them. "Call me Mara because the Almighty has made my life bitter. I went away full, but the Lord has brought me back empty. The Lord has brought bad things to me."

At the time, Naomi was too sad to see past her suffering. God was faithful to Naomi. She had come home empty, but God filled her life again with blessings and joy. You can read more about that in Ruth's story.

We all face hard things sometimes. Maybe you've already had some tough times. They can be as simple as failing a test or as complicated as living with a chronic illness like diabetes. Or maybe, like Naomi, someone you love has died — a parent, a brother or sister, a grandparent, a friend, or a favorite teacher.

You can choose to turn your pain or grief over to God. You can trust him to provide what you need to get through it. God is always good. He's faithful to walk through tough times with you and to help you get through them.

From GOD'S Heart

Trust in the LORD with all your heart and lean not on your own understanding; in all your ways acknowledge him, and he will make your paths straight.

—Proverbs 3:5–6

I will trust in the Lord's goodness even in
the tough times when I don't understand
why bad things happen.

Dear God . . .

Dear heavenly father, I confess I can't always
see your purpose for me. Help me in difficult times to remember how much you love
me. Please guide me as you guided Naomi.
Amen.

Check THIS Out

In Latin *levir* means "husband's brother." In a levirate marriage, if a husband died and left his wife without a son, his brother would take the widow to be his wife. The first son she had would carry on the name of her dead husband. The continuation of a family name was important in the Jewish culture. You can read more about it in Deuteronomy 25:5–10.

The name *Naomi* means "pleasant" or "my delight." The name *Mara* means "bitter." Both names fit Naomi at different stages in her life and places in her spiritual journey.

The Moabites, the people group Naomi's daughters-in-law were from, descended from Lot, Abraham's nephew.

Chapter 11

Ruth's Family Ties

Read Ruth's story in Ruth 1:3–4:22.

Ruth was a Moabite woman who grew up in a people group and family who worshiped false gods. Then Ruth married into an Israelite family who had moved to Moab to escape a famine in their homeland.

Most likely, Ruth heard her husband's family talking about their homeland and about the one true God. Ruth probably heard many stories about God's faithfulness to the Israelites. She heard the story about God parting the Red Sea to save his people from the Egyptian pharaoh's army. She heard that God gave Abraham and Sarah a son in their old age. She heard about how God used Deborah and Jael to save the Israelites from evil King Jabin.

When Ruth's husband died, she decided to follow her mother-in-law, Naomi, to Israel. Ruth wanted to care for

Naomi, who had lost her husband and two sons. Naomi had no one else to care for her, and she wanted to return to her homeland.

Ruth and Orpah, Naomi's other daughter-in-law, set off on the journey with Naomi. But when they reached the road that led to Judah, Naomi ordered them to go home to their mothers. Ruth and Orpah told her not to send them away, but again Naomi ordered them to leave her.

After Naomi's second speech, Orpah offered hugs all around and turned back toward the home she knew. Not Ruth. Ruth clung to Naomi and said, "Where you go I will go, and where you stay I will stay. Your people will be my people and your God my God. Where you die I will die, and there I will be buried."

Ruth loved Naomi with a love so deep that it led Ruth away from all she'd known and into a foreign land — into a land whose people didn't get along with her people. She chose Naomi's God over the false gods of the Moabites. She chose to serve Naomi even though Naomi had nothing to offer her.

Ruth and Naomi arrived in Bethlehem when the barley fields were golden and ready for harvest. "Let me go to the fields and pick up the leftover grain behind anyone who will let me," Ruth said.

According to the law and custom in Judah at that time, the poor could glean or gather for themselves whatever the harvesters missed. Though Ruth was a woman alone and a foreigner, she stepped out in faith to provide for her mother-in-law.

Boaz, the owner of the field, showed up while Ruth gleaned. He turned to the foreman of his harvesters and asked, "Whose young woman is that?"

The foreman said, "She is the Moabitess who came home with Naomi."

Boaz then spoke to Ruth. "Don't glean in any other field. Follow my servant girls. You will be safe here. And whenever you're thirsty, get a drink from the water jars."

He spoke with kindness and care. Ruth bowed. "Why are you being so kind to a foreigner?"

Boaz said, "I've been told about all you've done for your mother-in-law since the death of your husband. How you left your father and mother and your homeland and came to live with a people you didn't know. May the Lord, the God of Israel, bless you."

At mealtime Boaz invited Ruth to have bread with him and his harvesters. Ruth ate all she wanted and had some left over. When she left to gather more barley, Boaz told his men to pull stalks from their bundles and leave them for Ruth to pick up. Ruth carried an unusually large amount home to Naomi.

"Where did you glean today?" Naomi asked. "Blessed be the man who noticed you."

"In the fields of Boaz," Ruth said.

"Boaz is our close relative. He's one of our kinsman-redeemers." Naomi realized then that the Lord hadn't stopped caring for her. The exact field Ruth gleaned from that day belonged to her husband's relative Boaz.

Restored to faith and once again hopeful, Naomi began to share more of the Israelites' beliefs and customs with Ruth. Then one day Naomi told Ruth what to do next, and Ruth did as her mother-in-law suggested.

Ruth presented herself to Boaz to be his wife. Ruth was a risk-taker. Her new faith in God had given her boldness and courage.

"The Lord bless you," Boaz said. "I'm kin, but there is a kinsman-redeemer nearer than I. In the morning, I'll give him a chance to step up and redeem you. If he's not willing, I'll do it." Boaz poured six measures of barley into Ruth's shawl before he sent her back to Naomi.

The other relative told Boaz he could marry Ruth. So he did. And Ruth became pregnant.

God blessed Ruth for her faithfulness to God and to Naomi. Ruth discovered God's loyal and loving nature. God gave Ruth a new people, a new home, a new husband, and a son to carry on Naomi's family name.

Can you think of someone in your family who shows you God's love? An aunt or cousin, sister or grandparent, parent or teacher who models faith in God and loyalty to you?

Like Ruth, you can be a loving friend to your family members. Are you getting to know stepsisters or stepbrothers? Do you have a grandparent living in your home? Or maybe your situation involves a parent who doesn't know Jesus. Can you think of ways to show them the loyal and loving nature of God?

From GOD'S Heart

A friend loves at all times.

—Proverbs 17:17

I will be a loving friend and a
friend to the friendless.

Dear God . . .

Thank you, Lord, for my friends. Thank you,
Lord, for being my loyal and loving friend.
Help me to be a good friend too. In Jesus's
name, amen.

Check THIS Out

A kinsman-redeemer was responsible for protecting and caring for needy members of his extended family. He was supposed to provide an heir for a brother or any other male relative who had died and left a widow.

Remember Rahab? She was a Canaanite who placed her faith in God and also left her people to live among God's chosen people — the Israelites. Rahab married Salmon, and many Bible scholars believe Boaz, the man who married Ruth, was Rahab's son. Rahab and Ruth were both mentioned in Jesus' family tree. Read Matthew 1:5. Ruth was King David's great-grandmother.

The books of Ruth and Esther are the only books in the Bible named after women.

Chapter 12

Hannah's Promise

Read Hannah's story in 1 Samuel 1:1–2:11, 18–21, 26.

Hannah's husband Elkanah, like other men in her time, had another wife. The other wife, Peninnah, competed with Hannah for Elkanah's attention. And Peninnah had something Hannah couldn't give her husband—children. People placed a lot of importance on having children back then.

Peninnah loved to bug Hannah about not having any children.

Every year Hannah and her family traveled to worship in the temple in Shiloh. On those trips, it was especially hard for Hannah to avoid Peninnah's insults. Peninnah's meanness hurt Hannah so much she'd cry and not eat. Her husband said, "Hannah, why are you weeping? Why don't you eat? Don't I mean more to you than ten sons?"

Standing in the temple, Hannah humbled herself before God. Hannah prayed to the Lord in her heart with her lips moving. "O Lord Almighty, if you'll see your servant's misery and give me a son, I'll give him to the Lord for all the days of his life."

Eli the priest was in the temple, and he noticed Hannah praying and weeping. He saw that her lips moved, but she didn't speak. Eli said to her, "How long will you keep on getting drunk?"

"I'm not drunk," Hannah said. "I'm sad. I have been pouring out my soul to the Lord. I have been praying out of my great anguish."

Eli relaxed. Then he blessed Hannah. "May the God of Israel give you what you have asked of him." After this, Hannah's face was no longer downcast.

The next morning Hannah and Elkanah and the rest of his family traveled back home. Soon Hannah became pregnant and had a son she named Samuel, which means "asked of God" in Hebrew.

In those days, people had no way to keep milk from souring, so mothers nursed their children for three or more years. Hannah stayed home and nursed her son until he was weaned. She told her husband, "After he is weaned, I will present him to the Lord and he will live at the temple always."

After Hannah weaned Samuel, she took him to the temple at Shiloh, the place where she had cried out to God, and where God had heard her prayer and answered it. Hannah knew where her blessing had come from. She understood her son was on loan from God, and she kept her promise to God.

Each year Hannah traveled to Shiloh to worship, and each year she sewed Samuel a new robe to wear while he ministered there. Each year Eli the priest blessed Elkanah and his wife, saying "May the Lord give this woman children to take the place of the one she gave to the Lord."

God blessed Hannah and Elkanah with three more sons and two daughters. Meanwhile Samuel "continued to grow in stature and in favor with the Lord."

Hannah's promise to give her son to God for his purposes shows her heart's motive for asking for a son. It wasn't just so she could be a mother. She also wanted God to use her son to fill Israel's need for a godly leader. Her love for God was most important to her — not what she could get from God.

Often, God works in different ways from what we expect. Hannah knew that. Like Hannah, you can take your sadness to God and cry out to him. You can trust him to answer your cry, even if it's not the answer you expect. He knows what's best for you.

From GOD'S Heart

Let us then approach the throne of grace with confidence, so that we may receive mercy and find grace to help us in our time of need.

—Hebrews 4:16

I will take my problems to God and
seek his grace in times of trouble.

Dear God ...

Lord God, you have proven yourself faithful
and trustworthy. Please give me the grace to
trust you. Help me to pray out of a deep love
for you. For Jesus's sake. Amen.

A linen *ephod* was a garment worn by priests who served in the Lord's sanctuary. The sleeveless pullover was usually hip length and different from the ephod worn by the high priest. The little robe Hannah made for Samuel every year was sleeveless and stopped at his knees. He wore it between his undergarment and the ephod.

Check THIS Out

At the time, a Levite priest served in the temple from age 25 to age 50, but Hannah gave Samuel to God as soon as he was weaned to serve for the rest of his life. You can read more about it in Numbers 8:23–26.

Hannah's son Samuel became a prophet and Israel's last judge. He anointed both Saul and David as Israel's first kings.

The name Hannah means "grace or favor." In her sadness, Hannah learned more about God's grace. And through Hannah's son Samuel, God showed his grace to the nation of Israel.

Chapter 13

Abigail's Appeal

Read Abigail's story in 1 Samuel 25:1–42.

Imagine you're at home in the desert of Maon, west of the Dead Sea. You're married to a rancher of sheep and goats who is one of the richest men in the area. His name is Nabal, which means "fool." And, unfortunately, his name fit his character. Welcome to Abigail's life.

David, one of the nation's most powerful men, was camped out on Nabal's property in Carmel with six hundred of his men. It was shearing time. And Nabal had a thousand goats and three thousand sheep — plenty of meat to share.

David sent ten of his men to Nabal to deliver a message. "Long life to you. Good health to you and your household." David's men started the conversation by blessing Nabal and his family. "It's sheep-shearing time," the men said. "When your shepherds were with us we didn't mistreat them. The whole time they were at Carmel none of your goats or sheep went missing, so please give these young men and your son David whatever you can find for them."

Nabal puffed up. "Who is this David? Why should I take my bread and water and the meat I've slaughtered for my shearers and give it to his men?"

Nabal was a prideful and selfish man. It didn't matter to Nabal that David and his men had been good to him and helped guard his animals and had kept them from harm.

When the men returned to David with Nabal's answer, David was very angry. He told his men to sword up. David put on his sword too. Then he took four hundred men and headed toward Nabal's home.

One of Nabal's servants told Abigail that her husband had hurled insults at David's men after David and his men had protected them. He told her that David was getting ready to kill Nabal and all the men in Nabal's household for these insults.

Abigail wasted no time. She rose above her circumstances and took charge. Abigail ordered presents for David to be loaded onto donkeys — two hundred loaves of bread, two skins of wine, five sheep, a basket of roasted grain, one hundred raisin cakes, and two hundred pressed fig cakes. Then Abigail climbed onto her own donkey and headed toward David and his men.

When Abigail found David, she slid off her donkey, humbly bowed at David's feet, and begged him to listen to her. "Pay no attention to that wicked man Nabal,"

Abigail said. "Since the Lord has kept you from taking revenge and shedding blood, please forgive your servant's meanness. You fight the Lord's battles. Don't let any wrongdoing be found in you as long as you live."

Abigail appealed to David's sense of justice and showed concern for his integrity. She understood that David needed to protect his good name because God had plans for him.

David said to Abigail, "Praise the Lord who sent you today. Bless you for your good judgment and for keeping me from shedding blood this day." David accepted the gifts Abigail had brought with her. "Go home in peace," he said, "I've heard your words and granted your request."

Abigail's humility calmed David's anger. David changed his mind about punishing Nabal for his foolish treatment of him and his men.

Abigail took control of a dangerous situation and acted according to her faith in God. It took courage to go out to meet David, humility to plead with him, and wisdom to say what she said to the future king of Israel. Her wisdom kept David from sinning. God used Abigail to save many lives.

When Abigail returned home, Nabal was drunk. Abigail waited until the next morning to tell her husband she'd gone out to make things right with David. When she told him, his heart failed. He died ten days later.

After David heard of Nabal's death, he asked Abigail to marry him. She did.

When you're in the middle of difficult circumstances—a friend betrays you or a parent is too busy for you or your teacher doesn't understand you—you're the one who chooses your reaction and response. Like Abigail, you can place your trust in God and choose to develop a godly character—one of humility, generosity, understanding, wisdom, and calm judgment.

From GOD'S Heart

She [a wife of noble character] speaks with wisdom, and faithful instruction is on her tongue.

—Proverbs 31:26

I will seek God's wisdom and
speak in his wisdom.

Dear God . . .

Dear Jesus, thank you for being my peace-keeper. Help me to recognize danger and act wisely according to your will. Amen.

In 1 Samuel 25:24–31, Abigail's speech to David was one of the longest speeches given by a woman recorded in the Bible.

Check THIS Out

The name *Abigail* means my "father's joy." In the toughest of circumstances, Abigail found joy in God, her heavenly Father.

Chapter 14

Huldah's
Message

Read Huldah's story in 2 Kings 22:3–23:3.

King Josiah became king when he was eight. He ruled for thirty-one years. In the eighteenth year of his reign, King Josiah sent his secretary, Shaphan, to the temple of the Lord to deal with some money issues. When Shaphan was there, the high priest Hilkiah told him that he had found the book of the law in the temple. The book of the law tells about God's plan and is now part of the Old Testament in our Bible. Hilkiah gave the book of the law to Shaphan to bring back to King Josiah. The king's secretary read it to the king.

King Josiah was so upset by the words that he tore his robes. "The Lord is angry because we have not obeyed the words of this book," he said to the priest, the secretary, and three other men. "Go ask the Lord about the message written here."

Do you know where the men went to interpret the words?

To ask a woman. Though it was unusual in those days for a woman to speak for God, the king's men hurried to a house in the Second District of Jerusalem—Huldah's house.

Huldah was a prophetess. God used Huldah to explain the meaning of his words. These men of the temple and the king's house knew that Huldah was someone they could trust to interpret the words of God.

Huldah told the men God was angry and would bring disaster on this place and its people. They had turned their backs on God and worshiped false gods. God's anger would burn against this place, but because the king humbled himself and responded to the Lord, God would spare King Josiah from having to see the destruction of his land and its people. He would be buried in peace.

That had to be a hard message to deliver to the king's men. A powerful king could destroy Huldah for being the messenger of such devastating news. She could've been afraid and let her fear stop her from fulfilling God's purpose in her life. Instead she spoke the word of the Lord with courage.

The men returned to the king and told him what Huldah said. King Josiah called together all the leaders of Judah and Jerusalem and then joined them in the temple. After King Josiah read the Scriptures to them and told them of Huldah's interpretation, he made a promise to follow the Lord and to keep his commands. King Josiah removed all the idols from the temple.

God used Huldah to speak to the heart of King Josiah and to the leaders of Judah and Jerusalem.

If you were sitting at Huldah's table sipping pomegranate tea and munching almonds, she'd probably say, "Girlfriend, don't be shy or become lazy because of your young age, where you live, or for any other reason. Take a stand for God's Word, and be ready to tell people about God and his holy ways."

From GOD'S Heart

Be on your guard; stand firm in the faith; be men of courage; be strong.

—1 Corinthians 16:13

I will be a girl who stands firm
in my Christian faith.

Dear God . . .

Lord God, thank you for your truth. Please give me the courage to live it and share it. Amen.

Check THIS *Out*

$\mathcal{A}$ prophetess is a female prophet, a woman God uses to interpret and deliver his Word.

Huldah, Miriam, Deborah, and Anna all served God as prophetesses.

Huldah listened to God with her ears and with her heart. She paid attention to what God was doing and what he wanted her to tell others about him and for him. You can listen to God with your ears and with your heart. Are you ready for God to speak to you through the Bible and through people who know him and love him?

Today we have God the Holy Spirit to guide and help us. You can read more about the Holy Spirit in John 14:26; 15:26; and 16:7–15.

The name *Huldah* means "weasel." That's probably not something you want to be called. But it comes from a word that refers to the weasel's quick movement, which means to "glide swiftly" or "to move smoothly and quickly." That fits Huldah because she was quick to deliver God's message to the king's men.

Chapter 15

Vashti's Stand

Read Vashti's story in Esther 1:1–21.

Vashti seemed to have it all. Her very name meant "lovely." And Vashti was lovely. She also had a grand title: Queen Vashti. Her husband was the mighty King Xerxes who ruled over 127 provinces from India to Cush.

Vashti and the king were wintering at the citadel of Susa—the winter home of the Persian kings. In his third year as king, Xerxes hosted a banquet for his nobles and officials and military leaders and princes. For one hundred eighty days, the king showed off his great wealth and his glory.

Then he gave a seven-day banquet in the palace garden for people of every class, from the least to the greatest. And this wasn't your ordinary garden. Hangings of white and blue linen were fastened with cords of white linen and purple material attached to silver rings on marble pillars. Gold and silver couches sat on mosaic pavement of marble, porphyry, mother-of-pearl, and other beautiful stones. Servants served wine in goblets of gold.

Because it was improper in Persian culture for men and women to be entertained in the same place, Queen Vashti hosted the women in the palace.

On the last day of the banquet, the king was drunk and commanded his seven eunuchs to go and bring the queen to him. He wanted to put Vashti on display like a trophy. The king's men crashed Vashti's party and delivered the king's message to her.

What would she do?

He was the king, and he usually treated her very well. Vashti did enjoy a lot of nice things and special privileges because of her position as queen. But Vashti chose to tell the king, "No way." She refused to parade around in front of a bunch of drunken men.

Vashti's refusal wounded King Xerxes's pride, and he threw a fit. The king took his concerns about law and justice to the men who served him. "Queen Vashti didn't obey my command," he told them. "According to law, what must be done to her?"

One of them said, "Queen Vashti messed up big time. All women will learn she said no to you, and if you don't do something drastic to her, we'll all lose control of our women."

King Xerxes kicked Vashti out of the palace. She could never enter the king's presence again. Vashti lost her crown, her position in society, her home, and all the nice things that came with it. But she didn't lose her values.

Vashti didn't lower herself to the king's drunken level. She didn't give away her dignity. Yes, it was a high price to pay, but Vashti left the palace with her self-respect intact.

How important are material things to you? Do you value the latest fashions, designer electronics, and iffy friendships more than your reputation? Are they more important to you than your godly character? More important to you than your faith in God and making decisions that please him?

Are you willing, like Vashti, to give up temporary and material things to do the right thing?

From GOD'S Heart

A good name is more desirable than great riches; to be esteemed is better than silver or gold.

—Proverbs 22:1

I will choose integrity over human praise and material things.

Dear God . . .

God, thank you for giving me your name through Jesus. Thank you for making me your daughter. Help me learn your ways and remain loyal to you. In Jesus's name, amen.

Check THIS Out

*P*orphyry is purple volcanic rock that formed large crystals.

Mother-of-pearl is the hard inside layer of an oyster shell.

A *citadel* is an armed castle or well-protected fort.

Eunuchs were men who no longer had their external genitalia. Because of that, kings trusted them with the women in the royal palace.

Real Girl Talk

Real beauty is beauty people can recognize even when they can't see your face. They can talk to you on the phone or read an email from you and know you have beauty of character. True beauty is a gorgeous heart that seeks to know God and to follow his ways.

If Vashti sat around with you and your friends while you all plaited, or braided, each other's hair, I think she'd talk to you about boys. Yep, boys. And modesty.

She'd tell you that sometimes we girls are tempted to wear things and do things for boys because we think that will make them like us more. We might be talked into showing off our bodies with inappropriate clothing. Vashti would probably tell you not to parade around like that just to get some guy to notice you and like you more — even if he's king of his own little universe.

It's super important to be decent in the way you dress and act around boys. You don't want to give them the wrong idea. You don't want them to think they can treat you like a piece of property, the way King Xerxes treated Vashti.

Chapter 16

A Crown for Esther

Read Esther's story in Esther 2:5–7:7; 9.

I imagine Esther wondered more than once about God's plans for her.

Esther's Hebrew family had been captured and exiled to a foreign country. When Esther's parents died, her older cousin Mordecai raised her in a city of Susa in Persia. And as if all that wasn't enough of a challenge, Xerxes, the king of Persia, needed a new queen.

What did that have to do with Esther? Many pretty girls were taken to the king's palace for a beauty contest. And Esther was one of them. After twelve months of beauty treatments and special food, Esther decked out in a fancy gown and glided in to meet King Xerxes.

When the king saw her, he said, "This is the one!" Then he crowned her Queen Esther.

Later, Esther's cousin Mordecai angered Haman, who was the king's second-in-command. Mordecai, who held a high position in the king's service, refused to bow before Haman. Mordecai said, "I only bow before God."

Haman talked King Xerxes into signing an order for all the Jews in the city to be killed on a certain date. Neither Haman nor the king knew Esther was Mordecai's cousin and that she was also a Jew.

Mordecai gave one of King Xerxes' eunuchs a message for Esther. "Go to the king and beg for mercy."

If Esther went to speak to the king without him calling for her, she could be killed. If Esther didn't go to the king, her cousin and the other Jews in the country would be killed.

In another message to Esther, Mordecai said, "Who knows, maybe you became queen for such a time as this?"

Had Esther become queen as part of God's plan? Did God plan to use Esther to save her people from certain death?

Esther sent her answer to Mordecai through a eunuch named Hathach. "Gather all the Jews in Susa together. Don't eat or drink for three days and nights," Esther said. "Pray for me. I'll pray too. Then I'll go to the king even though it is against the law. And if I die, I die."

At that time in the Jewish culture, prayer — communicating with God — was the focus of fasting. After fasting and praying for three days, Esther slipped into her fancy queen duds and headed for the king's throne room. King Xerxes was glad to see her.

Phew! Her life was spared.

Esther invited the king and Haman to two banquets with her. After the second banquet, the king told Esther he'd give her anything she wanted—even half of his kingdom. Half of everything King Xerxes owned was a lot of land and jewels and animals.

But would the king save her cousin? Would King Xerxes save the other Jews Haman planned to kill? Would he save her?

Queen Esther told the king about Haman's plan to kill her people. King Xerxes ordered Haman to be killed. Then the king appointed Esther's cousin Mordecai to be his new second-in-command.

Esther could've gone for the loot—half of the king's kingdom—or she could've let fear get the best of her. She could've chosen to keep quiet about being a Jew. Instead Esther trusted God to help her fulfill his plan for her life. "For such a time as this" Esther had been chosen as queen. Every girl is born for a purpose. Esther was called on to step up and do the hard thing. You might be too.

From GOD'S Heart

"I know the plans I have for you," declares the Lord, "plans to prosper you and not to harm you, plans to give you hope and a future."

—Jeremiah 29:11

I will trust God's plans for me.

Check **THIS** *Out*

Esther's outside beauty treatments included six months of being slathered with oil of myrrh and six months of aromatherapy with perfumes and cosmetics. Myrrh is a gum or sap that comes from trees and shrubs in Eastern Africa.

What was Esther's inner beauty treatment for the job God had for her? Prayer and trust. Esther prayed for three days and nights. She trusted God with her life.

The name *Esther*, her Babylonian name, means "star." That fits Esther because she was a bright star in the drama of Jewish history.

Her Hebrew name, *Hadassah*, means "myrtle." Myrtle is a sweet-smelling Mediterranean floral shrub with dark-colored berries. After all those beauty treatments, I'm sure Esther smelled at least as sweet as the flowers on a myrtle bush.

PART 2

New Testament Girls

Chapter 17

Mary's Encounter

Read Mary's story in Luke 1:26–38; 2:1–20, 41–52;
Matthew 1:16–25; 2; Mark 3:20–35; John 2:1–12;
19:25–27; Acts 1:12–14.

Mary was a teenager who came from a poor family in Nazareth, a small village in Galilee. She was betrothed, or engaged, to Joseph, a carpenter, and soon they'd marry and start a family. But in less time than it took to dip a goatskin bottle into a spring and fill it with water, Mary's simple life turned into a divine adventure.

One day the angel Gabriel stood in front of Mary and said, "Greetings, you who are highly favored. The Lord is with you."

Mary was surprised and troubled by the angel's greeting. If this was an angel of the Lord, why was he visiting her? What could it mean?

Before Mary's dry mouth could form words, Gabriel spoke again. "Don't be afraid, Mary, you've found favor with God. You'll give birth to a son. Name him Jesus because he'll be great — the Son of the Most High."

"I'm a virgin. How can I have a baby?" Mary asked. Mary had never been with a man, not like she would be when she married Joseph.

The angel said, "The Holy Spirit will make it happen. Even your relative Elizabeth will have a child in her old age. She who was said to be barren is in her sixth month. Nothing is impossible with God."

"I'm the Lord's servant," Mary said. "May it be to me as you have said." With faith and humility, Mary said yes to God's call upon her life.

Then the angel left her.

Do you think Mary wondered what other people would think? Do you think she worried about what Joseph, her friends, and her family would say and do? It must have been difficult to share her unusual news.

Mary was pregnant, and Joseph wasn't the baby's father. According to the law, Joseph could've had Mary judged publicly by her friends and family. If he had, she could've been stoned and killed by rocks.

Joseph didn't want to disgrace Mary in public. A betrothal could only be broken by a divorce process. Joseph thought about getting a divorce, but then the angel of the Lord visited him in a dream. "Joseph, don't be afraid to take Mary home as your wife. She has conceived from the Holy Spirit. She'll give birth to a son, and you're to name him Jesus. He will save his people from their sins."

Joseph woke up and took Mary home to be his wife, but Mary remained a virgin until after Jesus was born.

Mary was very pregnant when the Roman emperor, Caesar Augustus, decided to gather information he could use to grow his military and charge taxes. Caesar ordered people to go back to their hometowns to register. For Joseph, that meant at least a three-day trip from Nazareth to Bethlehem. So he and Mary set off on the journey.

When they finally arrived in Bethlehem, Mary was ready to have her baby. But a stable was the only place they found for lodging. In that day, a stable was probably more like a cave. That's where Mary gave birth to Jesus, the Son of God. She wrapped him in strips of cloth and laid him in a manger, which was a feeding trough for animals.

What would it be like to be the mother of Jesus, who was a boy but also God's Son? Mary loved her son. She fed him when he was hungry. She took care of him when he was sick. She wanted to keep him safe. But Jesus wasn't like other children. Mary didn't always understand her son. Like the day at the temple...

Mary, Joseph, Jesus, and other relatives had traveled to the temple in Jerusalem for the feast of the Passover. On their way home, Mary couldn't find twelve-year-old Jesus anywhere among their group. He wasn't with the other children. And he wasn't with his aunts or uncles.

Mary and Joseph traveled back to Jerusalem and found Jesus in the temple. He was sitting with the teachers of the law, listening to them and asking questions. Was Mary surprised to see her son in deep discussions with the leaders? She must've been proud of him. But she was a mother who'd been worried sick about her son. And she was angry. "Son, why have you treated us like this?" she said. "Your father and I have looked high and low for you."

Jesus said, "Didn't you know I had to be in my Father's house?"

Though, at the time, Mary didn't understand what Jesus was saying, she did treasure his words in her heart and thought about them while her son grew.

Later, Mary spent time with Jesus and his disciples. Mary may have been a widow then, since we don't hear about Joseph in any more of the scenes with Mary and Jesus. They were at a wedding feast together in Cana when the family ran out of wine. That was a serious problem, so Mary went to Jesus and said, "They have no more wine." Mary turned to the servants and said, "Do whatever he tells you." Mary knew Jesus had knowledge and power no one else had.

Jesus told the servants to fill the six stone jars with water. They did, and then he told them to take a sample of the water to the master of the banquet. When they did, the master said it was excellent wine. Jesus had turned water into wine. And Mary had witnessed her son's first miracle. She had to know he was truly the Son of God, Immanuel, God with us!

Later, she joined her son on his journey to Jerusalem. In the Bible, Matthew, Mark, Luke, and John all say that Mary was at the cross. Her sister stood beside her as Mary watched Jesus hang on a cross like a thief or a murderer. When Jesus saw his mother there and his beloved disciple

John, he said, "Dear woman, here's your son." He said to John, "Here's your mother." From that moment on, John took Mary into his home and cared for her.

Mary had to watch her son die, but she also saw her son after he'd been raised from the dead. And Mary continued to be part of the ministry Jesus started here on earth.

God wants you to be his loving and faithful servant, ready to be used for his glory. Are you listening for God's voice? Are you willing and ready for him to direct you according to his purposes?

From GOD'S Heart

Jesus looked at them and said, "With man this is impossible, but with God all things are possible."

—Matthew 19:26

I will believe that all things are possible with God.

Dear God . . .

O God, because of your great grace all things are possible. Thank you. Please help me live in the peace and joy you give me through your grace. In Jesus's name, amen.

A Jewish *betrothal* was much more binding than a typical engagement in our society. If a woman was betrothed—pledged to be married—she was called a wife even though she wasn't actually married yet. A betrothal could only be broken by divorce. To divorce, a betrothed couple had to sign legal papers.

Check THIS Out

Mary may have had seven children: Jesus, James, Joses, Simon, Judas, and two daughters whose names we don't know.

Chapter 18

Elizabeth's Visitor

Read Elizabeth's story in Luke 1:5–25, 39–80.

*W*hen Elizabeth saw her relative Mary walking toward her house, she thought her heart might burst with joy. Mary had come all the way from Nazareth to the hill country outside Jerusalem to see her.

Like Sarah of the Old Testament, Elizabeth had lived through years of infertility. The Bible says Elizabeth and her husband Zechariah were well along in years. Gray probably streaked Elizabeth's hair. But it didn't matter to God. Now Elizabeth was six months pregnant with a son. Elizabeth had no doubt that this baby was a gift from God. Her husband, Zechariah, was a priest. One day when he came home from the temple, he couldn't speak. He had to scribble on a wax tablet to tell Elizabeth the amazing story that follows.

While Zechariah performed his duties in the temple, an angel of the Lord appeared. "Don't be afraid, Zechariah; your prayer has been heard," the angel of the Lord said. "Your wife, Elizabeth, will have a son. Name him John. He'll bring many of the people of Israel back to the Lord their God. He'll go before the Lord to prepare the people for the Lord."

"How can I be sure of this?" Zechariah asked. "I'm an old man, and my wife is well along in years."

"I am Gabriel," the angel said. "I stand in the presence of God, and I've been sent to speak to you and to tell you this good news. Now because you didn't believe my words, which will come true at their proper time, you'll be silent and unable to speak until John's birth."

Elizabeth believed God's promise of a child, and she soon became pregnant.

And now Mary, a teenager, stood before her. Elizabeth knew something was different about Mary. The baby inside Elizabeth's womb jumped, and she shouted, "You are blessed among women. Blessed is the child you'll bear. But why am I so blessed that the mother of my Lord would come to see me?"

Mary's belly hadn't grown yet, and Mary hadn't told Elizabeth about the baby she carried. But Elizabeth knew. Not only that, but Elizabeth knew it was the Lord Jesus that Mary carried in her womb. The Holy Spirit had spoken the truth to Elizabeth's heart. She believed in God's plan and rejoiced with Mary. And Elizabeth must've been a huge encouragement to Mary.

The Bible only says that Elizabeth and Mary were relatives. It doesn't specify whether Elizabeth was Mary's aunt or if they were cousins. Through the angel, Gabriel, God had told Mary of Elizabeth's pregnancy. He brought them together to love and encourage one another in their pregnancies.

Mary stayed with Elizabeth for about three months, probably until after Elizabeth's son was born. God had a plan for their lives, and he took care of them.

It wasn't an accident that Elizabeth, a woman up in years who had never had a baby, was finally able to conceive. And it wasn't a coincidence or an accident that a few months later, God chose Mary, a virgin, to conceive his Son, Jesus, through the work of the Holy Spirit. God had a divine plan. And the circumstances and timing were all part of it. God chose Elizabeth's son, John the Baptist, to prepare the way for the coming Messiah, Jesus.

The circumstances in your life aren't just coincidences or accidents either. God has his hand on you. And he can use any circumstance or situation for his divine purposes and for your good. Like Elizabeth, you can trust God and be sensitive to his Holy Spirit. You too can learn to recognize God at work in your life and in the lives of your friends and family. And just as Elizabeth encouraged Mary, you can encourage the people God places in your life.

From GOD'S Heart

Do not let any unwholesome talk come out of your mouths, but only what is helpful for building others up according to their needs, that it may benefit those who listen.

—Ephesians 4:29

I will think and listen before I speak so
I can be an encourager.

Dear God . . .

Father God, your ways are amazing. Thank you for the way you fit the pieces of my life together in your plan for me. Help me see you at work in the lives of my family and friends and be an encouragement to them. Amen.

In Hebrew, the name *Elizabeth* means "consecrated to God." Elizabeth was dedicated and set apart in her faith.

Check THIS Out

Elizabeth was a descendent of Moses's brother Aaron.

Mary and Elizabeth's Baby Development Notes

God our creator shapes every child in the womb. Every life — every baby — is a miracle.

After the mother's egg is fertilized, human chromosomes or DNA are present, and a new life has begun. By day six, the embryo is already made up of 250 cells.

At four weeks, even though the embryo is tiny, the cells are already specialized, or getting their instructions for what their jobs will be. Some cells will become the brain, others will become skin and hair, others will form the respiratory and digestive systems, and others will become bones or muscles.

At six weeks, the embryo looks like a tadpole, but it is only half the size of a pencil eraser. The legs are not well developed, so it is mostly head and body. By now, the doctor can hear a heartbeat.

At twelve weeks, the embryo is called a fetus because it has developed its basic structure. All the organs are formed; they just need to grow. The fetus may measure between 1.5 and 3 inches from head to bottom (legs are curled up) and weigh about an ounce.

At twenty weeks, the doctor, using an ultrasound, can tell if the fetus is a boy or a girl. The fetus can suck its thumb, and the mother can feel it moving around.

At twenty-four weeks, the fetus may weigh a little over one pound. It can hear sounds and respond by moving. The mother may feel baby hiccups, which feel like a tiny jerking motion.

At twenty-eight weeks, the fetus may weigh over two pounds. Its lungs are fully formed, and it could survive if it was born now.

At thirty-two weeks, the fetus is moving around a lot. Between now and its birthday, the fetus gains about half of its weight.

At thirty-six weeks, the fetus is getting ready for its birthday. Its brain develops quickly in the last weeks. The space is tight so the fetus doesn't move around much anymore. The fetus's head is usually pointing down.

At thirty-seven weeks, the baby is full term and ready to be born.

Chapter 19

Anna's Call to
Prayer

Read Anna's story in Luke 2:22–38.

Anna didn't always do what everyone else did. Every country and generation has its own customs. During that time, it was the custom that a Jewish widow without children move back into her parents' house until another man wanted to marry her. But that's not what Anna did.

Anna was married only seven years when her husband died. Instead of doing what others would've done, she moved into the temple in Jerusalem. The Bible says Anna never left the temple. She worshiped God night and day, fasting and praying. Anna was a prophetess.

King Herod had rebuilt the temple, and it was way different from our churches, even different from most Jewish temples today.

Made of white marble and decorated in gold, the temple was more like a city than a church. Huge walls surrounded the area, which was about the size of twelve soccer fields. Watchtowers stood at the corners of the wall. Rabbis taught on wide steps that led to gates. Jews and Gentiles came to the temple to pray, to offer sacrifices, to pay their temple tax, and to discuss religious issues with rabbis. This was where Anna lived and served God. She likely bunked in one of the many rooms on the temple grounds.

When Anna's husband died and left her alone, Anna became a woman who talked about the coming Messiah and then about Jesus, the Messiah, to all who would listen. She was a woman who talked to God night and day. Anna lived a life of prayer in an active relationship with God.

Mary and Joseph took baby Jesus to Jerusalem to present him to the Lord. It was written in the Law that every firstborn male was to be consecrated to God. Mary and Joseph came to offer a sacrifice of two doves or pigeons. Anna was a senior citizen when Joseph and Mary showed up at Herod's Temple with the baby Jesus.

"Jesus." Anna's lips trembled with joy as she spoke his name. This was the Messiah she'd been waiting for. Praying for. Talking about. Anna gazed into the tender eyes of the one who came to save her, her people, and the world from sin.

We're never too young or too old to thank God for his goodness and speak to others about Jesus, God's holy Son.

Whether bad things happen — like your best friend moves away or your parents get divorced, or good things happen — like you win the state spelling bee or your family takes a dream vacation, you can live like Anna did. You don't have to live in a church or in a temple, but you can be a girl who prays night and day. You can tell the people around you about Jesus who is Savior to all who believe in him.

From GOD'S Heart

Do not be anxious about anything, but in everything, by prayer and petition, with thanksgiving, present your requests to God.

—Philippians 4:6

I will talk to God about the bad and the good things in my life and thank him for being my great God.

Dear God . . .

Lord God, I'm so glad I can talk to you and that you listen to me. Please teach me how to pray more for other people. In Jesus's name, amen.

Anna was from the tribe of Asher, one of Jacob's twelve sons.

Check THIS Out

The name *Anna* is the same name as *Hannah* in the Old Testament, which means "gracious." Someone who is gracious is kind and forgiving. Anna was gracious. She spent her life worshiping God through prayer and then sharing the good news of Jesus with others.

If you were standing in the temple courts with Anna, she might have something to say about 1 Corinthians 6:19–20. "Do you not know that your body is a temple of the Holy Spirit, who is in you, whom you have received from God? You are not your own; you were bought at a price. Therefore honor God with your body."

Anna knew oodles about the Jewish temple. Even with her eyes closed, Anna could probably find all the areas where women were allowed. And I think she'd love that God thinks of our bodies as temples for his Holy Spirit. If she read those verses with you, she might tell you that God wonderfully made your body. She'd probably tell you to take special care of your body because it belongs to the King of kings and Lord of lords. And that taking care of God's temple — your body — is an act of worship, a way we can thank God for creating us in his image.

Chapter 20

A Cure for the
Woman in the Crowd

Read the woman in the crowd's story in
Matthew 9:20–22; Mark 5:24–34; Luke 8:43–48.

Imagine not being able to be with your family or friends because you're considered unclean. You're an outcast. Not because of anything you've done, but because of an inner wound you have no control over. That's what life was like for the woman who was "subject to bleeding," also called the "woman in the crowd."

This woman had been subject to bleeding for twelve years. No doctor could heal her. Any attempts to cure her only made the problem worse. Twelve years is a long time to lose that much blood. She must have been anemic and weak. And according to Jewish law at the time, she was ceremonially unclean, which meant everyone avoided her. They believed if they touched her or anything she touched, they too would become unclean. No one wanted anything to do with her.

She wasn't allowed in the temple. No one could touch chairs or other things she'd touched. The Bible doesn't mention her family. She couldn't get married or have kids. She was sick and alone. And she'd spent all her money on doctors and trying to find a cure. Nothing had worked. She was too weak to work, and no one would hire her anyway.

With no money to live on, no strength to keep going, and no friends to encourage her, she was desperate for healing.

Then one day as she hovered at the edge of a crowd at the lake, perhaps at Capernum, she saw Jesus. She had heard about Jesus, and she believed if she could just touch his cloak, she'd be healed. Jesus was her only hope. Ignoring her pride, fear, and embarrassment, she pressed into the crushing crowd.

Her fingers brushed the fabric of Jesus' cloak, and in that instant, her bleeding stopped. She knew she'd been freed of her suffering.

What would you have done?

She slipped back into the crowd.

Then Jesus turned and asked, "Who touched my clothes?"

The disciples must've thought Jesus was joking. Peter said, "You see all these people crowded against you. Lots of people touched your clothes."

"Someone touched me. I know power went out from me." Jesus kept looking around. Because he was

God, Jesus certainly knew who had touched him and why. Still, he wanted her to come forward and tell her story. He wanted the crowd to know she was no longer "unclean."

The woman stepped out of the crowd, fell at Jesus' feet, and told him of her illness and his healing touch.

"Daughter," Jesus said, "your faith has healed you. Go in peace, free from your suffering."

In Greek the word for *healed* also means "saved." Because of her faith in Jesus, he healed her from her physical illness and saved her spiritual being too. Jesus felt compassion for people suffering physically and didn't limit his work to spiritual healing. He also took care of their physical needs.

When Jesus called her *daughter*, he gave her worth and respect. She was now part of the family of God.

Faith requires risk. The woman in the crowd knew that. She risked being discovered and rejected, but her faith was greater than her fear. Like her, you can humble yourself and reach out to Jesus. You can allow Jesus to heal your wounded heart and to forgive your sins.

If you've never done that, maybe you're ready to reach out to Jesus right where you are today. You can ask Jesus to forgive your sins and be your Savior and friend.

From GOD'S Heart

The Lord is gracious and righteous; our God is full of compassion.

—Psalm 116:5

I will show God's great love to the
people he places in my life.

Dear God . . .

Father God, you're a loving and caring God.
Thank you for loving me. I want to show the
people around me your great compassion.
Please help me do that, Lord. In Jesus's name,
amen.

Because the theme of compassion is so important, it appears in the Bible as *compassion* or *compassionate* at least one hundred times. And God's great compassion is a theme in the book of Psalms.

Check THIS Out

A cloak is the outer clothing or robe Jewish men wore. Usually made of woolen cloth, the cloak wrapped around the man's body to help keep him warm.

Chapter 21

A Healer for Jairus's Daughter

Read Jairus's daughter's story in
Mark 5:21–24, 35–43; Luke 8:40–42, 49–56.

Jairus, a synagogue ruler, had a sick daughter. As a synagogue ruler, Jairus was responsible for looking after the building, conducting services, and maintaining order at the temple. He was a powerful man, but he was powerless to heal his sick daughter.

Jairus heard Jesus had the power to work miracles, and Jesus was coming to their town. While his daughter lay at home dying, Jairus left to find Jesus. When he did find Jesus, Jairus hurried into the crowd, fell at Jesus' feet, and begged Jesus to come to his house and heal his daughter.

Jesus started to follow Jairus home, but stopped when a woman who was bleeding touched his cloak. This kept Jesus from getting to Jairus's house immediately.

The Bible doesn't describe Jairus's daughter's illness. She must have been very ill when her father left to find Jesus. Did she know her father was gone? That he'd been gone longer than expected? Did she think it would be too late for her by the time her father arrived with Jesus?

While Jesus still spoke to the woman in the crowd, someone came from Jairus's house and told him, "Your daughter is dead. Don't bother the teacher anymore."

Jesus heard and said to Jairus, "Don't be afraid. Believe, and she'll be healed."

When Jesus arrived at the house, mourners cried for Jairus's daughter. Jesus only let Peter, John, James, and the girl's father and mother inside the room with him. Perhaps because he knew they were the only people who believed he could heal her. He didn't want them to tell anyone what he did. Meanwhile, the mourners continued to wail, and Jesus said, "Stop wailing. She's not dead. She's asleep."

The mourners laughed at him. They believed the girl was permanently dead because they didn't believe Jesus could bring her back to life.

Jesus reached out and held the girl's hand. "My child," he said, "get up."

Immediately, her spirit returned to her body. Having received her miracle, the girl stood up and walked around. Do you know what Jesus did next? He told her parents to give her something to eat. Jesus made sure all of her needs were met.

Jesus wants us to trust him to do the same for us. You can give your health and your very life to Jesus. And like

Jairus's daughter, you can accept Jesus's gift of grace. You can let him heal you. Maybe your heart has been broken by the loss of a friend who moved away or by the rejection of someone you love. Maybe you need to accept Jesus's hand and let him help you up, out of sadness, grief, or anger.

Or maybe, like Jairus's daughter, you've seen Jesus work a miracle in your life or in the life of a family member. Have you thanked Jesus for his presence in your life? Have you praised him for who he is — God's Son and your Savior?

From GOD'S Heart

I have set the LORD always before me. Because he is at my right hand, I will not be shaken.

—Psalm 16:8

I will remember that the Lord is
always with me and accept his hand
of love and help.

Dear God . . .

Dear God, you are my provider. You know my needs. And I'm so glad you take care of me and will never leave me. Thank you. Amen.

_W_hat kinds of things did girls do during Jesus' time on earth?

At a young age they began to help with household chores like sweeping, fetching water, and helping take care of the animals. Jairus was a religious leader. He and his family had more money than some, so his daughter may not have done as many chores as other kids. Though most children didn't have many toys to play with, some had toys made out of clay. Jairus's daughter may have had a clay doll.

When someone died during Jesus's time on earth, it was the custom to hire professional mourners. Since the time between Jairus's daughter's death and Jesus's arrival at the house was short, there may not have been time to get professional mourners there. Those that Jesus told to stop wailing might've been other family members, family friends, or neighbors.

You wouldn't have found any low tops, bare bellies, or short shorts on respectable girls in Jesus's day. Their fashions included tunics in wool, cotton, or linen worn to the ankles. Because Jairus's daughter was part of a wealthier family, she may have worn a more colorful tunic than most other girls. And her tunic may have had a V-neck with embroidery along the edges.

And forget tennies. Girls and women wore simple leather sandals, some with wooden soles.

Chapter 22

Mary of Bethany's Choice

Read Mary of Bethany's story in Luke
10:38–42; John 11:1–45; 12:1–8.

A woman named Mary, not the mother of Jesus, lived in a village called Bethany about two miles out of Jerusalem. She became known as Mary of Bethany. She lived with her sister, Martha. Their brother, Lazarus, also shared the house with them. The Bible mentions that Mary, Martha, and Lazarus were all friends of Jesus, and he visited their home when he traveled through Bethany.

One of Mary of Bethany's favorite things to do was to sit at Jesus's feet and listen to his teachings. Spending time with Jesus was one way Mary showed her love and deepened her faith in him.

One time when Jesus was at their home, Mary sat at Jesus's feet while Martha prepared a meal for the guests.

Martha asked Jesus to tell Mary to help her with the work.

Jesus said to Martha, "You are worried and upset about many things, but only one thing is needed. Mary has chosen what is better, and it will not be taken away from her." Listening to Jesus was the better choice for Mary right then.

Another time, Lazarus became ill when Jesus was not there. Mary and Martha sent a messenger to tell Jesus of their brother's illness. Although Jesus loved Mary, Martha, and Lazarus, he waited two days before he left for Bethany. By then, Lazarus had died. The disciples warned Jesus that it wasn't safe to go to Bethany because not long before that Jews in that area had tried to stone him. But Jesus and his disciples traveled back to Bethany so Jesus could "wake" Lazarus.

When Mary reached Jesus, she fell at his feet and said, "Lord, if you'd been here, my brother wouldn't be dead."

Jesus wasn't surprised that Lazarus was dead. He knew that he didn't make it back in time. But Jesus loved Mary and her family, and so he wept with Mary.

Jesus and his disciples followed Mary, Martha, and the other mourners to the tomb, which was a cave with a stone placed across its entrance. "Take away the stone," Jesus said.

When the disciples took away the stone, Jesus looked up and said, "Father, thank you for hearing me. You always hear me." Then Jesus called out in a loud voice, "Lazarus, come out."

Lazarus walked out of the tomb with his hands and feet still wrapped with linen and a cloth around his face.

The next time Jesus went to Bethany, he was on his way to Jerusalem for the Jewish Passover. Again, he visited Mary, Martha, and Lazarus. Martha prepared a dinner in Jesus's honor. Mary was a woman of few words, but her actions spoke much about her tender heart and her love for Jesus. Mary took a pint of pure nard, an expensive perfume, and poured it on Jesus's feet. After she had anointed his feet, Mary dried them with her hair.

Though some grumbled about her extravagant choice, Mary didn't show concern for what others thought or said. She focused on her Lord Jesus. She used the perfume to anoint Jesus to prepare for his coming death. Mary's gift of anointing Jesus with perfume showed she'd listened to Jesus and believed him.

Like Mary, focus on Jesus. Spend time in prayer and read and reflect upon Scripture before you take action.

From GOD'S Heart

"I am the resurrection and the life. He who believes in me will live, even though he dies; and whoever lives and believes in me will never die. Do you believe this?"

—John 11:25–26

I will believe what Jesus says and live like I believe him.

Dear God . . .

Dear Jesus, please forgive me for those times when I don't show my love for you. I do love you. Thank you for all you are to me and all you do for me. I want to show you how much I love you, please teach me how. Amen.

The house Mary lived in with her sister Martha didn't have fans or air conditioning. The walls, probably made of mud bricks or stones and sticks, were built thick to keep the house cool in the summer and warm on winter nights.

Check THIS Out

When the sun sank in the sky there weren't any light switches to flip at Mary's house. She and Martha and Lazarus probably visited with Jesus in the light of an oil lamp made of clay or metal.

Nard was a perfume made from oil taken out of the root of a plant mainly grown in India.

Chapter 23

Martha's
Sider Trouble

Read Martha's story in Luke 10:38–42; John 11:1–12:3.

Martha owned the house in Bethany where Jesus went to teach, rest, and receive nourishment. Jesus spent time there with people he loved and who loved him. This included Martha, her sister, Mary, and their brother, Lazarus.

During one of Jesus's visits, Martha was working hard to prepare a good meal for Jesus and his disciples. Mary, on the other hand, was in with the men, sitting at Jesus's feet like she had nothing else to do. The harder Martha worked, the more frustrated she became. The more frustrated she became, the angrier she became. Martha stomped into the room where Jesus and the others sat. She had had it and went straight to the Lord to complain.

"Lord," Martha said, "don't you care that my sister has left me to do the work all by myself? Tell her to help me."

Martha wanted Jesus to take her side and fix the problem by telling Mary to get off her lazy fanny and get to work. But she learned that the Lord doesn't always give the answer we want or expect.

"Martha, Martha," Jesus answered, "you're worried and upset about many things, but only one thing is needed. Mary has chosen what is better, and it won't be taken away from her."

That wasn't the answer Martha wanted. Mary had chosen "what is better"? To sit at Jesus's feet and learn from him was better than serving him? Better than doing things for him?

Martha wasn't wrong to show her love for Jesus through serving him with her gift of hospitality. It wasn't wrong for her to cook a nice meal for Jesus and his disciples. So where had Martha gone wrong?

Martha had a bad attitude. Jesus didn't scold Martha for wanting to serve him well, but for her attitude. She was distracted in the preparations to serve him. She started worrying about all she wanted to do to make everything perfect. She had failed to focus on who it was she wanted to serve.

Instead Martha focused on herself. What she wanted. What she needed to do. And what she couldn't do by herself. Then she decided it was Mary's fault. She became distracted and angry.

As it turned out, Martha didn't have sister trouble; she had Martha trouble. But here's what's so great about Martha: She had a relationship so close to Jesus that she didn't have to hide her feelings and frustrations. She was free to be herself with Jesus.

Martha complained to Jesus, and he scolded her for her bad attitude. But then Martha changed her heart and attitude and actions.

After Jesus raised Martha's brother, Lazarus, from the dead, Jesus again visited Martha's home. And Martha prepared another meal for Jesus and his followers. But this time she didn't protest. Martha's attitude about serving had changed. The dinner was her gift to Jesus, not her duty. And she accepted Mary's way of serving God.

Martha was the practical one. And when her attitude was right, there was great value in her service. Jesus wants us to focus on him no matter what we're doing.

Martha took her troubles directly to her Lord. You can too. You can be honest with God about what you're feeling and thinking. Instead of spreading your complaints through your family or among your friends, you can take them directly to Jesus.

From GOD'S Heart

Whatever you do, whether in word or deed,
do it all in the name of the Lord Jesus, giving
thanks to God the Father though him.

—Colossians 3:17

I will love God first, and then serve him
out of my love for him.

Dear God . . .

Thank you, God, for your patience. Even when I'm frustrated or lonely, angry or confused, guilty or afraid, happy or sad, you meet me where I am. Help me learn to give all of my feelings to you. Help me focus on your love for me and on my love for you. Amen.

Check THIS Out

What kind of meal might you serve Jesus if he came to your house for supper or dinner today? Martha probably fixed a pot of vegetable stew or a barley stew with lentils. She served it with bread and finished the meal with fruit, such as grapes, figs, or dates.

The name *Martha* means "lady," which fits this Martha because she was the lady of the house.

Chapter 24

A Widow's Offering

Read the widow's story in Mark 12:41–44; Luke 21:1–4.

A widow walked alone into the Court of Women at the temple in Jerusalem. We don't know much about her. The Bible tells us she is poor and refers to her, not by name, but as a widow.

In her hand, the widow held the two smallest coins in circulation in Palestine. Though they were small and worn, that's all she had. But she was glad to give all she had to the God she loved.

Soon the Jewish people would celebrate Passover. Worshipers from all over Israel packed into the temple. It took great faith for the widow to offer her last pennies, but she did. She dropped the two very small copper coins into one of the receptacles in the temple.

A few days earlier, Jesus had ridden a donkey down the Mount of Olives into Jerusalem. And he was at the temple that day, watching the crowd place their money in the temple treasury. He watched rich people drop in large amounts. And he watched the poor widow put in her two small copper coins. Jesus called his disciples to him and said, "This poor widow has given more than all the others."

Didn't it make more sense that the more money a person put in the more they gave? What could the temple do with two tiny coins?

Yes, but Jesus doesn't think that way. His ways and thoughts are higher than ours.

"They all gave out of their wealth," Jesus said, "but she gave out of her poverty. She put in everything she had to live on."

That was faith. Giving everything she had to God. The widow had given her poverty to God and trusted him to take care of her. And Jesus noticed. He saw the deepness of the widow's love for him in her gift.

What do you have in your hand? Maybe you think you don't have much to give Jesus. But no gift is too small if you offer it to God out of a heart of love for him. Jesus looks beyond your circumstances — what you have and don't have to give. He looks into your heart. Your willingness to give what you have matters to him. Your heart attitude toward God is what's most important to him.

Maybe you sing or write songs or play an instrument. Are you willing to let God use your music to lead others in worship?

Maybe you have extra toys or books or clothes you can give to a needy child in your town.

Maybe you bake, and you could make something special for a lonely widow in your church or neighborhood.

Is there something you possess that is more important to you than your relationship with God? Is it your wardrobe? Maybe a doll collection or a collection of movies? Is it a friendship with someone who has a bad influence on you? God wants to be first in your life. Most important to you. And he deserves to be. God is worthy of our love and devotion.

When you love God with all your heart and offer him all you have, you learn to trust him more and more. And your relationship with God grows stronger.

Are you stingy with what God has given you, or are you grateful and generous? Think about what God has given you. Make a list or your talents, abilities, and possessions. Offer them all to God as a love gift, and look for ways to use what you have for his glory.

From GOD'S Heart

If the willingness is there, the gift is acceptable according to what one has, not according to what he does not have.

—2 Corinthians 8:12

I will generously give out of a heart grateful for all God has given me.

Dear God . . .

Dear heavenly father, you gave me so much when you sent your son Jesus to die for my sins. You've given me everything you have. Thank you. Help me be more generous to you and to others. For Jesus's sake, amen.

Check THIS Out

Because both men and women were allowed in the Court of Women, that's where the temple treasury was located.

Thirteen trumpet-shaped receptacles, or containers, hung on the wall in the temple treasury. They were smaller at the mouth and wider at the bottom.

Real Girl Talk

If you were sitting under an olive tree with the widow, she'd probably share her experience with being judged by people who didn't really know her. As humans we tend to judge others by what's on the outside. But God sees your heart and judges you according to what's in your heart.

Base your identity—your sense of self-worth—on your relationship with God, not on what you see in the mirror. Or on what other people say about you.

Chapter 25

A Forgiven Woman's
Fragrant Faith

Read the forgiven woman's story in Luke 7:36–50.

Luke tells the story of a woman who was known for her sin, but he doesn't give her name or identify her sins. It doesn't seem to matter for the sake of the story—just that she had done something everyone else thought was pretty bad.

A Pharisee named Simon invited Jesus to dinner. He had heard about Jesus because Jesus had been preaching in Judea and the surrounding areas. Word had gotten out about Jesus healing the blind, the lame, the deaf, the lepers, and those with evil spirits. Many religious leaders were unhappy about Jesus's growing popularity. They had been in control, and they wanted to keep it that way. They didn't like his talk about grace and forgiveness.

Perhaps this Pharisee, a religious leader named Simon, hadn't invited Jesus to dinner to learn from him, but to trick him. He might have been looking for a way to stop Jesus and his growing popularity.

While Jesus reclined at the Pharisee's table with his feet out in front of him, the woman known for her sin showed up with an alabaster jar. She had probably heard Jesus talk about how, through grace, one could be forgiven and lead a new life. When she heard that Jesus was at the Pharisee's house, she came to show Jesus her love and gratitude.

The woman stood at Jesus's feet and wept, her tears cleaning his dusty feet. After she wiped his feet dry with her hair, she kissed them, and then broke open an alabaster jar and poured perfume on Jesus's feet.

The Pharisee was someone who loved the law and was proud of his good works. He thought to himself that if Jesus were a prophet, he wouldn't have let this unclean woman touch him. He must have had a disapproving look on his face because Jesus said, "Simon, I have something to tell you."

"Tell me, teacher," the Pharisee said.

"Two men owed money to a certain moneylender. One owed him five hundred denarii, and the other fifty. Neither of them had the money to pay him back so he canceled the debts of both. Now which of them will love him more?"

Simon said, "I suppose the one who had the bigger debt canceled."

"You're right." Jesus turned to the woman, but spoke to Simon again. "Do you see this woman? I came into your house. You didn't give me any water for my feet, but she wet my feet with her tears and wiped them with her hair. You didn't give me a kiss, but this woman hasn't stopped kissing my feet. You didn't put oil on my head, but she poured perfume on my feet. Her many sins have been forgiven—for she loved much. But he who has been forgiven little loves little."

Then Jesus spoke to the woman. "Your sins are forgiven," he said. "Your faith has saved you; go in peace."

Jesus didn't look at the nature of her sin as the Pharisee and the others there did. He saw her faith. In a humble expression of her love, she'd demonstrated her gratitude for Jesus's forgiveness.

The Pharisee apparently thought he was better than the woman because he hadn't committed the sins he saw in her. But his self-righteousness was a sin. His pride and judgment were his sins. He did not ask for forgiveness or demonstrate his love for Jesus as she had.

In God's eyes, sin is sin. It doesn't matter what it is or who knows about it. God sees everything we do and hears everything we say. He knows when we sin, when we judge unfairly, and when we have sincerely asked for forgiveness.

That's what is so amazing. God knows you better than anyone else and still loves you and forgives you when you confess your sin and ask for his forgiveness. Others may reject you for what you do or don't do, but Jesus forgives you. And because of his love and forgiveness, you can live in peace with God. That's grace.

From GOD'S Heart

All have sinned and fall short of the glory of
God, and are justified freely by his grace through
the redemption that came by Christ Jesus.

—Romans 3:23–24

I will confess my sin to God and accept
his grace and forgiveness.

Dear God . . .

Dear God, thank you for sending your perfect Son, Jesus, to die for my sin. Every day,
help me see my sins and confess them to you
and accept your great forgiveness. In Jesus's
name, amen.

Check THIS Out

An alabaster jar
was a sealed flask
made of stone. It held
enough ointment for one appli-
cation. To use the contents,
you'd have to break the long neck off the jar.

A denarius was a coin worth about one day's wages.

In Jewish culture, because guests traveled by foot on dusty roads, it was the custom to offer your guests water to clean their feet. It was also customary to greet one another with a holy kiss, as an act of respect and unity.

Chapter 20

Mary Magdalene's Deeper Healing

Read Mary Magdalene's story in Mark 16:1–8;
Luke 8:1–3; John 19:25; 20:1–18.

When Mary Magdalene first met Jesus, she was sick. Mary didn't have a cold or chicken pox or cancer. Instead, seven demons, or devils, lived inside her.

Mary's second name, *Magdalene*, came from "Magdala," the name of the small village where she lived on the west side of the Sea of Galilee. So she was Mary from Magdala, or Mary Magdalene.

One day Jesus visited Mary's village and made the seven devils leave Mary Magdalene.

After that, Mary left Magdala to travel with Jesus and the others who followed him. The Bible says she and other women helped finance the work of Jesus and his disciples. The women provided the money so Jesus could travel from the shores of the Sea of Galilee to the city of Jerusalem to teach people about God the Father.

Mary Magdalene's money may have come from an inheritance from her father. Or she may have been the widow of a man who had left her some money. The Bible doesn't say where her money came from. But it does say Mary Magdalene followed Jesus all the way to the cross. She watched Jesus die for her sins, for your sins, and for my sins.

Would Mary Magdalene ever get over the sadness of watching Jesus die? How would she live with never seeing Jesus again?

Early Easter morning, Mary Magdalene and two other women hurried to the tomb where the Roman soldiers buried Jesus. Because it was a Jewish custom to cover bodies with oils and spices, the women carried lotions and spices with them. As they walked, they wondered who would roll the huge stone away from the tomb. But when the women arrived, the stone lay beside the empty grave. And Jesus's body was gone.

Mary Magdalene ran back to town to find the disciples. "They've taken the Lord out of the tomb," she told them, "and we don't know where they've put him."

Simon Peter and the other disciples followed Mary Magdalene back to the empty grave. After the disciples returned home, Mary Magdalene stood outside the tomb crying. When she turned around, she saw a man she thought was a gardener.

"Woman," he said, "why are you crying? Who is it you're looking for?"

"Sir, if you've carried him away, tell me where you've put him and I'll get him."

"Mary."

As soon as Mary Magdalene heard the man speak her name, she knew it was Jesus. He was alive! No one had taken his body away. Jesus had risen from the dead. Just as he'd said he would.

"Rabboni!" Mary cried out in Aramaic. She called Jesus Teacher. He had taught her much about God's amazing love, grace, and mercy. Jesus was her Savior, friend, and teacher.

Jesus told Mary Magdalene to go tell the others he was returning to his Father and her Father, to his God and her God.

Mary Magdalene hurried to the disciples with the news. "I've seen the Lord."

Mary Magdalene was the first human to see Jesus alive after his death on the cross. She'd served Jesus with her heart, her finances, and her feet, and God rewarded her faithfulness.

Like Mary Magdalene, you can believe Jesus is God's son and learn from him. You can believe he cares for you. You can follow Jesus in your heart and with your feet, learning to walk in his perfect ways.

From GOD'S Heart

Many nations will come and say, "Come let us go up to the mountain of the LORD, to the house of the God of Jacob. He will teach us his ways, so that we may walk in his paths."

—Micah 4:2

I will learn more about Jesus's character
and follow his lead.

> ## Dear God . . .
>
> Dear Jesus, I want to be like you. Please teach
> me how so I can teach my friends and family
> about you and your ways. Amen.

How did Mary
Magdalene travel
from town to town with
Jesus and the others? Mostly on
foot. Back then, they didn't have
cars or trains or planes. They walked. She probably wore
through lots of pairs of sandals.

Check THIS *Out*

The name *Mary* means "bitterness." Before Jesus
chased the devils out of Mary, she was bitter and
unhappy. Her second name, *Magdalene*, from *Magdala*,
means "tower." After Jesus healed her, Mary followed
Jesus and, like a tower for her world to see, she helped
others find Jesus.

Chapter 27

Living Water for the
Samaritan Woman

Read the Samaritan woman's story in John 4:1–42.

There was a woman who lived in Sychar, a small village in Samaria. The Bible calls her the Samaritan woman.

Because the woman needed water, she trekked to Jacob's well. People usually drew water at the end of the day. But not her. Not that day. She wasn't like most other women. She may have wanted to avoid their stares and gossip. It was about noon when she carried her jar to the well.

Still, when she arrived at the well, she wasn't alone. A man rested on the ground nearby. The man was Jesus. Jesus had left Judea and was headed for Galilee. He had to go through Samaria on the way. Jesus stopped and sat down by Jacob's well. While Jesus rested, the disciples went into town to get food.

The Samaritan woman could see that the man sitting near the well was a Jew. Orthodox Jews from the north usually went out of their way to avoid Samaria because the Jews and Samaritans didn't get along. So what was he doing here?

"Will you give me a drink?" the man asked.

"You're a Jew and I'm a Samaritan woman," she said. "How can you ask me for a drink?"

The popular belief at that time was that all Samaritans were *unclean*. So the Jews believed they would also become unclean if they drank out of a cup handled by a Samaritan. Jesus was a Jew, but his heart was not ruled by human fears, rules, and habits. His heart was ruled by God the Father.

"If you knew the gift of God and who asks you for a drink," Jesus said, "you would've asked him and he would've given you living water."

"Sir, you have nothing to draw with, and the well is deep. Where can you get this living water?"

Jesus said, "Everyone who drinks this water will thirst again, but whoever drinks the water I give him will never thirst. The water I give him will become in him a spring of water welling up to eternal life."

Jesus wasn't talking about plain old well water. He was talking about salvation and eternal life with God. Jesus was the living water. He was the only one who could satisfy the deep thirst in the Samaritan woman's soul.

"Sir," she said, "give me this water so I won't get thirsty and have to keep coming here to draw water."

Jesus said, "Go, call your husband and come back."

"I have no husband," she said.

"You're right. You have no husband. You've had five husbands, but the man you live with now isn't your husband."

Since this man — this Jew — knew the truth about her, she thought he was a prophet. "Sir," she said, "I know that Messiah is coming."

Jesus said, "I am he. I'm the promised Messiah."

This was the only place recorded before Jesus's trial where Jesus specifically said he was the Messiah — the Christ.

Leaving her water jar, the Samaritan woman hurried back to town. She shared her story about Jesus with others and said, "Come."

Many of the Samaritans from Sychar followed her and found Jesus. They put their faith in him and then begged him to stay with them and teach them more. Jesus stayed two days in their town, and because of his words many more became believers.

This woman was God's choice to tell others about Jesus and his gift of eternal life.

Jesus knew the Samaritan woman needed more than just water from the well that day. He knew she needed forgiveness for her sins. And he knew she needed to know that God loved her that much.

God knows your needs too, even before you do. And he doesn't decide your importance because of your color, your ethnic background, the money in your piggy bank, how often you attend church, or the good things you do. He looks into your heart. He sees if you've placed your faith in his son, Jesus Christ.

And like the Samaritan woman at the well did, you can believe Jesus is who he says he is and you can have a personal relationship with him and tell others so they can know him too.

From GOD'S Heart

Jesus answered, "I am the way and the truth and the life. No one comes to the Father except through me."

—John 14:6

I will tell others about Jesus and show them the way to a personal relationship with God.

Dear God . . .

Father God, thank you for providing a way for me to know you. Thank you for Jesus. Please show me how to share Jesus with my family, friends, and with all the people you place in my life. In Jesus's name, amen.

Fetching water was a daily chore. If there were older girls in

Check THIS Out

the family, they were usually the ones to fill goatskin bags at a nearby spring or well.

Real-Girl Walking Tips

If one of our Bible girls was here getting ready to go for a walk with you, she might give you the following tips on walking as a form of exercise.

1. Wear good walking shoes.
2. Apply a good sunscreen.
3. Grab a full water bottle for refreshing sips.
4. Before walking, stretch out your leg muscles to warm them up, especially if it's early in your day.
5. Take a walking buddy with you.
6. Pay attention to your surroundings.
7. Check out the beauty of God's nature as you walk, but also watch your step.

Chapter 28

A Miracle for Dorcas

Read Dorcas's story in Acts 9:36–43.

*D*orcas liked to sew, but she didn't have a fancy sewing machine with a buttonholer or a sleeve attachment. She sewed by hand in her home in Joppa, the main seaport of Judea, about thirty-five miles northwest of Jerusalem.

Dorcas was a disciple and belonged to one of the first Christian congregations. And one of her favorite ways to serve Jesus was to serve the poor in her community. The Bible says Dorcas always did good and helped the poor. Not just on Sundays or at Christmas time or when her church or the post office had a food drive. Sewing clothes for the needy was one way Dorcas helped.

When Dorcas became ill and died, many widows and others mourned her death. They washed her body and placed it in an upstairs room in her house along the Mediterranean Sea.

Two men from Dorcas's hometown went over to Lydda where the apostle Peter was preaching. They told Peter to come to Joppa at once. When Peter arrived at Dorcas's house, they took him upstairs to her room. The crying widows surrounded Peter, showing him the robes and other clothes Dorcas had made for the poor.

Peter sent them all out of the room. He knelt on the floor and prayed. Then he said, "Tabitha, get up."

Dorcas, whose name translated to *Tabitha* in Aramaic, opened her eyes. She saw Peter and sat up. She'd been dead, and now she was alive again.

Peter held Dorcas's hand and helped her to her feet. Then he called the believers and widows in to see Dorcas alive again. The miracle became known all over Joppa, and many people believed in the Lord.

God gave Dorcas more time on earth to praise his name. More time to use her heart and her hands to serve God and the poor in her community.

Like Dorcas, you can allow God to use your gifts, abilities, and talents to serve the poor and needy in the world. You can share your time and talent to let them know God loves them and cares about them. How will you show God's love? What can you do to serve the poor in your community?

From GOD'S Heart

If you spend yourselves in behalf of the hungry and satisfy the needs of the oppressed, then your light will rise in the darkness, and your night will become like the noonday.

—Isaiah 58:10

I will care for the poor as Jesus did.

Dear God ...

Lord, you see the needs of all people all around the world. Your heart breaks for them. Please show me the things that break your heart and give me a heart to serve the needy as Jesus did. Amen.

According to Jewish custom, if a dead person's burial was delayed for any reason, the body was to be laid in an upper room. Outside

Check THIS Out

the city of Jerusalem, they could wait up to three days before burial. Inside the city, burial had to take place on the day a person died.

The name *Dorcas* means "gazelle." A gazelle is a small, speedy antelope. That description could fit Dorcas. She was quick to see the needs of the poor and do what she could to meet them.

The town of *Joppa* is now called *Jaffa*. It is a suburb of Tel Aviv.

Chapter 29

God's Gift to Eunice

Read Eunice's story in Acts 16:1–5; 2 Timothy 1:1–5; 3:10–17.

What do you think is the most important job of a parent? What could be more important than loving or feeding a child or keeping a child safe? Several times in the Bible, Timothy's mom is held up by Paul as a great parent. Paul mentions her because she raised her son to know the holy Scriptures.

Eunice was a Jewish believer in Jesus Christ and also a mom. She was a mom who loved the Lord and wanted her son Timothy to know and love the Lord. His formal study began at age five, but Timothy learned early. From the time he was an infant, his mother taught him the holy Scriptures. Though she was married to a Greek unbeliever, Eunice raised her son Timothy in the Christian faith. And Timothy came to love the Lord and the Word of God.

The family lived in Lystra in the hill country of the area now called Turkey. The apostle Paul traveled there on his missionary journeys across Asia. The believers at Lystra, and at Iconium about twenty miles away, knew of Timothy's strong faith in Christ and spoke well of him.

Timothy was probably a teenager when Paul first met him and chose to take Timothy along with him on his second missionary journey. Timothy went from town to town with Paul and other missionaries. They crossed into Greece, taking the gospel into Europe for the first time.

Eunice lived in imperfect and probably difficult circumstances. She loved the Lord and studied the Scriptures, even though her husband didn't. Still, Eunice grew in her Christian faith and nurtured her son Timothy in that faith.

How about you? Do you live in imperfect and difficult circumstances? Maybe you believe in Jesus, but some of your family members don't, and they make it hard for you.

Today, if you were down at a stream helping Eunice wash the family's laundry, she'd probably talk to you about God's faithfulness. She'd probably tell you how her heart ached and leapt with joy at the same time as she watched her son leave home on his first missionary trip. Her words would likely run together in her excitement as she told you how God used her son Timothy to help grow the first Christian churches in the world.

Eunice was faithful to God, and she understood the importance of teaching her son God's truth. Like

Eunice, you can remain faithful to God in every circumstance, study the Bible on your own, and ask God to show you how to teach others in your family about him.

From GOD'S Heart

All Scripture is God-breathed and is useful for teaching, rebuking, correcting and training in righteousness, so that the man of God may be thoroughly equipped for every good work.

—2 Timothy 3:16–17

I will study the Bible, God's holy Word,
so that I can know God and learn to
love his holy ways.

Dear God . . .

Lord God, thank you for giving me your holy Word so I can know you and your holy ways. Help me be more regular in reading and studying the Bible and applying your truths to my daily life. For Jesus's sake, amen.

*D*uring Jesus's time on earth, the Scriptures only consisted of the Old Testament books. At first, the writings of the Old Testament were on separate scrolls written in Hebrew, and the Old Testament consisted of thirty-nine books. Later, the twenty-seven books of the New Testament were written in Greek. The books of 1 Timothy and 2 Timothy are part of the apostle Paul's letters to the Christian churches and to individual Christians in various cities.

In Greek, the name *Eunice* means "victorious." Because Eunice was faithful to teach her son God's ways, she experienced victory in her life.

Lydia's Riverbank
Prayer Meeting

Read Lydia's story in Acts 16:6–40.

*P*urple may have been Lydia's favorite color. She was a successful businesswoman who sold fine cloth. Lydia was a Gentile from Thyatira in Asia Minor. Thyatira was famous for its dying works and was the center of production of royal purple.

Lydia's job was to sell purple cloth, but she was also a worshiper of God. Lydia had a family to care for and a business to run. She was busy. Still, she set aside time in her busy schedule for God. But Lydia didn't worship God in a church building.

The law stated that a city needed ten reliable Jewish males before the city could have a synagogue. Since Philippi didn't have enough Jews to support a synagogue, the women worshiped and prayed at the river's edge.

The apostle Paul, along with Silas and Timothy, traveled to Philippi on one of their missionary journeys. On the Sabbath, they went out of the city gate to the place of prayer along the river's edge. There, the three missionaries sat with Lydia and the other women, and Paul preached about Jesus. He told them God was a holy God. That all people were sinners and fell short of God's holiness. Paul also told Lydia that Jesus was God's perfect Son, who had been crucified and had risen from the dead for love's sake. He did this so all people could receive forgiveness for their sins and have a personal relationship with God the Father.

That day Lydia believed in the Lord Jesus Christ and became the first recorded convert to Christianity in Europe.

Lydia had known there was a God, and she worshiped him. But, there on the riverbank with Paul, she learned the rest of the story. She heard and believed that she was a sinner who needed Jesus to be her Savior.

Paul hadn't planned to visit Philippi. But God had his own plan for Paul. And God's plan included Lydia, the other women, and all of Philippi and Europe. God wanted them to hear the good news of Jesus, so the Holy Spirit spoke to Paul through a dream and led him and Silas and Timothy to the women on the riverbank that Sabbath day.

Lydia was strong in her faith in Jesus. She was so enthusiastic that her whole household became Christians. Lydia invited Paul and his fellow missionaries to stay in her home. They stayed for several days, and Lydia's home became the center of Paul's teaching ministry in Philippi.

God had heard Lydia's prayers. Like Lydia, you can seek God through prayer. You can ask God to reveal himself to you, your family, your community, your country, and the entire world.

What about you? Do you only know of God because you've heard a family member talk about him or heard about him at church? Or do you have a real relationship with God through your own belief in Jesus?

From GOD'S Heart

Ask and it will be given to you; seek and you will find; knock and the door will be opened to you. For everyone who asks receives; he who seeks finds; and to him who knocks, the door will be opened.

—Matthew 7:7–8

I will continue to seek God and his holy ways.

Dear God . . .

Dear heavenly father, thank you for all you did so I can know you and have a personal relationship with you. I love you. Amen.

Check THIS Out

𝒫hilippi, a city in Eastern Macedonia in Greece, was a Roman colony named after Philip II, father of Alexander the Great.

Real-Girl Prayer Tips

Sometimes when we pray, it's good to close our eyes and fold our hands. Closing our eyes and folding our hands can help us ignore distractions and maybe even avoid them. But we can pray standing up or lying in our bed. We can pray out loud or quietly in our spirit. We can pray with tears of sadness or tears of joy. We can talk to God anytime and anywhere.

Chapter 31

Rhoda's Daring Role

Read Rhoda's story in Acts 12:1–19

Rhoda worked in a well-off residential section of Jerusalem. No, Rhoda wasn't an interior designer, a personal hair dresser, or even a dog walker. Rhoda was a servant girl who worked in the home of a woman named Mary. Yes, at that time, Mary was a popular name. This particular Mary was the mother of John Mark, the "Mark" who wrote the second gospel in the New Testament.

You might think Rhoda's job as a servant or a maid sounds kind of boring. Nope. Rhoda's story is one of drama, suspense, and humor. Her job wasn't all about dusting and mopping, or washing clothes in the river. The *Early Church,* the followers of the risen Christ Jesus, met secretly in Mary's house.

The Roman king, Herod Agrippa I, ordered the persecution of the early Christians, and he had the apostle Peter arrested for his faith. The king ordered that a squad of four men guard Peter around the clock. While Peter sat in jail, Mary, Mark, and others gathered in Mary's home and prayed for Peter's safe release from prison.

When a knock sounded on the door at the outer entrance, it was Rhoda's job to answer it. I think I would have at least hesitated to answer the door. Maybe refused. The church was, after all, being persecuted for their faith. One of their members was recently executed. Another member was imprisoned and, no doubt, facing the same fate.

Boring, no. Dangerous, yes. Despite any concerns Rhoda might have had about brawny Roman soldiers crashing their prayer meeting, she went to see who was knocking. She recognized the voice on the other side of the door.

Peter! Peter was free. He was safe. And he was there at Mary's house. More than a little excited, Rhoda didn't even open the door to let him in before running to tell the others of the wonderful news. "Peter is at the door!" she shouted.

"You're out of your mind," she was told.

If you had been one of those praying for Peter's release, would you have believed Rhoda? Knowing the evil intentions of the king, would you have thought it possible for Peter to have been freed?

The knocking persisted. I'm sure Peter wasn't comfortable waiting outside.

Rhoda kept insisting it was Peter.

The others finally did open the door to see for themselves. Astonished, they listened to Peter's amazing story. That night, the night before his scheduled trial, he'd been asleep between two soldiers, bound with chains. Two sentries stood guard at the entrance. Suddenly, an angel of the Lord awoke him. The chains fell off Peter's wrists. The angel told Peter to dress in his cloak and sandals, and he did. Peter followed the angel out of the cell. They passed the guards and went through the iron gate leading to the city, which opened by itself. They walked the length of one street, and the angel left Peter. That's when Peter realized he hadn't been dreaming and that the Lord had rescued him from Herod Agrippa's clutches.

Have you ever felt like what you do isn't important? Like your role in life doesn't matter?

It's so easy to look at what our friends and family members are doing and think what we do isn't as important.

For Rhoda, going to the door first that night allowed her to be the first person to learn of God's answer to prayer in Peter's life. When Rhoda recognized Peter's voice on the other side of the door, she knew God had heard their prayers and done a miraculous thing. Peter was freed as an act of God.

At times, God may call you to serve him in the spotlight where people see what you're doing and recognize its value. More often, God asks us to serve him on the sidelines, doing basic, even boring, tasks. He may ask you to do something as simple as opening a door for someone else. Serving him may be praying for missionaries or baking cookies for a lonely neighbor. The task may not bring with it drama, suspense, and humor, but then again, it just might.

What do you feel the Lord is calling you to do for him today?

From GOD'S Heart

And whatever you do, whether in word or deed, do it all in the name of the Lord Jesus, giving thanks to God the father through him.

–Colossians 3:17

I will serve God wherever I am with a
heart of thanksgiving.

Dear God . . .

Lord God, sometimes I don't like where I am or what I have to do. Please help me to trust you, knowing that you are with me always and working in ways that I may not see. For Jesus's sake, amen.

Rhoda worked in a home in Jerusalem. Thirty-three miles east of the Mediterranean, Jerusalem was by this time the largest city in the country of Judea and served as a religious and commercial center.

Check THIS Out

The Book of Acts in the New Testament is a study of the birth of the *early church*, a group of Jesus's followers. Acts tells us what happened after Jesus died and returned to heaven. The believers followed Jesus's command to go forth and preach the gospel to all, and they sent out missionaries like Paul, Barnabas, Timothy, and others. Acts is the book that tells the story of how the Christian faith spread to the whole world. And Rhoda had a daring role in God's exciting story.

Chapter 32

More Real Girl Talk

A thread runs through each one of our Bible-girl stories. Did you see the thread? God's great love is woven throughout the Bible and in each of our girls' stories. No matter which story you read, you can see God at work in the life of that Bible girl as God the Father, God the Holy Spirit, or God the Son, Jesus Christ.

Even in the lives of the Bible girls in the Old Testament, God the Father was preparing the way for Jesus. It started with Eve in the garden of Eden. When she and Adam disobeyed God, sin interrupted their relationship with him, a perfect God. But God so loves you and me that he had a plan to make the relationship right. That's where his perfect Son, Jesus Christ, came in. Born a human baby, Jesus grew up and took all our sin to the cross for us. He paid the price for our sin so we can enjoy a relationship with God. So we can have the Holy Spirit at work in our lives.

Check out what the Bible has to say about it.

For all have sinned and fall short of the glory of
God, and are justified freely by his grace through
the redemption that came by Christ Jesus.
God presented him as a sacrifice of atonement,
through faith in his blood.

—ROMANS 3:23–25

Sin—wanting our own way—is a human condition
that we all struggle with.

For the wages of sin is death, but the gift of God
is eternal life in Christ Jesus our Lord.

—ROMANS 6:23

Because of sin, your soul (your spiritual being) and my
soul are dead to God who is perfect and without sin. But
God still loved us and gave us the best gift of all. He sent
his perfect Son, Jesus Christ, to die on the cross for our sin.

For God so loved the world that he gave his one
and only Son, that whoever believes in him shall
not perish but have eternal life.

—JOHN 3:16

All we have to do is believe that Jesus is who God
says he is. If we put our faith in Jesus, even after our body
dies, our soul will live forever with God in heaven.

If we confess our sins, he is faithful and just and
will forgive us our sins and purify us from all
unrighteousness.

—1 JOHN 1:9

If we repent of our sins, God will forgive us and make
us clean because of what Jesus did for us.

Yet to all who received [Jesus], to those who
believed in his name, he gave the right to
become children of God.

—JOHN 1:12

If we believe Jesus is God's perfect son who died in
our place so we can have a relationship with God, and
if we receive Jesus as our personal savior, we become a
child of God.

Right where you are right now, you can talk to God.
You can make sure Jesus is at the center of your life story.
You can become a child of God. You can know that
when you die you will spend eternity with Jesus.

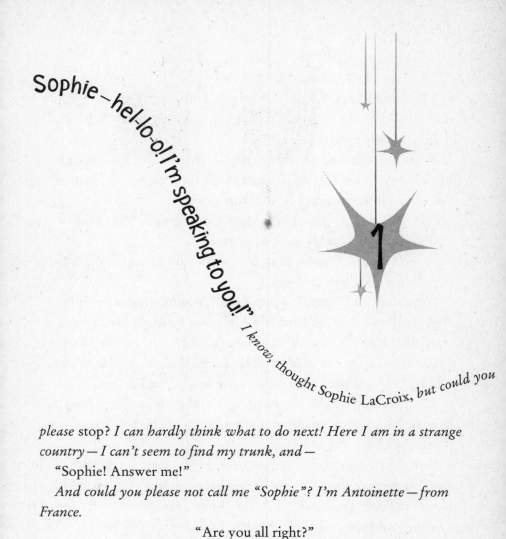

"Sophie—hel-lo-o! I'm speaking to you!"

I know, thought Sophie LaCroix, *but could you please stop? I can hardly think what to do next! Here I am in a strange country—I can't seem to find my trunk, and—*

"Sophie! Answer me!"

And could you please not call me "Sophie"? I'm Antoinette—from France.

"Are you all right?"

Sophie felt hands clamp onto her elf-like shoulders, and she looked up into the frowning face of Ms. Quelling, her sixth-grade social studies teacher. Sophie blinked her M&M-shaped eyes behind her glasses and sent the imaginary Antoinette scurrying back into her mind-world.

"Are you all right?" Ms. Quelling said again.

"Yes, ma'am," Sophie said.

"Then why didn't you answer me? I thought you were going into a coma, child." Ms. Quelling gave a too-big sigh. "Why do I even plan field trips?"

Sophie wasn't sure whether to answer that or not. She had only been in Ms. Quelling's class a month. In fact, she'd only been in Great Marsh Elementary School for a month.

"So answer my question," Ms. Quelling said. "Do you or don't you have a buddy in your group?"

"No, ma'am," Sophie said. She wasn't quite sure who was even *in* her field trip group.

"You're in the Patriots' Group." Ms. Quelling frowned over her clipboard, the skin between her eyebrows twisting into a backwards S. "Everybody in that group has a buddy except Maggie LaQuita — so I guess that's a no-brainer. Maggie, Sophie is your buddy. LaQuita and LaCroix, you two can be the La-La's."

Ms. Quelling rocked her head back and forth, sending her thick bronze hair bouncing off the sides of her face. She looked *very* pleased with her funny self.

But the stocky, black-haired girl who stepped up to them didn't seem to think it was the least bit hilarious. Sophie recognized Maggie from language arts class. She drilled her deep brown eyes into Ms. Quelling and then into Sophie.

Don't look at me, Sophie wanted to say out loud. *I don't want to be La-La either. I am Antoinette!*

Although, Sophie thought, *this Maggie person could fit right in. She looks like she's from a faraway kingdom, maybe Spain or some other romantic land. She can't be "Maggie" though*, Sophie decided. *She had to be Magdalena, a runaway princess.*

Magdalena glanced over her shoulder as she knelt to retrieve the leather satchel, stuffed with her most precious possessions —

"So are you getting on the bus or what?"

Maggie's voice dropped each word with a thud. She hiked her leather backpack over her shoulder and gave Sophie a push in the back that propelled tiny Sophie toward the steps.

"Sit here," Maggie said.

She shoved Sophie into a seat three rows back from the driver and fell in beside her. In front of them, the other four Patriots fell into seats and stuffed their backpacks underneath. They twisted and turned to inspect the bus. Somebody's mother stood in the aisle with Ms. Quelling and counted heads.

"I have my six Patriots!" she sang out, smiling at their teacher. "Two boys, four girls!"

"Eddie and Colton, settle down!" Ms. Quelling said to the boys seated between the two pairs of girls. Eddie burrowed his knuckles into Colton's ball cap, and Colton grabbed the spike of sandy hair rising from Eddie's forehead.

"Dude," Maggie muttered. "I'm stuck in the loser group again."

Sophie squinted at Maggie. "I thought we were the Patriots."

"They just call us that so we won't *know* we're in the loser group."

"Oh," Sophie said.

She craned her neck to see over Colton and Eddie's heads and get a look at the other two Patriots. The girl with butter-blonde hair squirmed around in her seat to gaze longingly toward the back of the bus.

SHE hates being in the loser group too, Sophie thought. Actually she was pretty sure the girl, whose name she knew was B.J., hadn't lost anything but her usual knot of friends. She and three other girls always walked together as if they were attached with Superglue.

B.J.'s lower lip stuck out like the seat of a sofa. Next to her sat a girl with a bouncy black ponytail. Ponytail Girl tugged at the back of B.J.'s T-shirt that read *Great Marsh Elementary School* — the same maroon one they were all wearing. Sophie had selected a long skirt with daisies on it to wear with hers, as well as her hooded sweatshirt. She always felt most like Antoinette when she was wearing a hood.

B.J. leaned further into the aisle. The only thing holding her onto the seat was the grip Ponytail Girl had on her.

"B.J., you're going to be on the floor any minute," said Chaperone Mom. "How about you scoot yourself right back up next to Kitty?"

"What?" B.J. said. She whirled around to Kitty and yanked her shirt away.

"B.J., what's the problem?" Ms. Quelling said from further down the aisle.

B.J.'s sofa lip extended into a foldout couch. "If I could just be with my friends in the Colonists Group — "

"And if ants could just have machine guns, we wouldn't step on them!" Ms. Quelling said.

"But they don't," Maggie said.

"Exactly." Ms. Quelling stretched her neck at B.J. over the top of the clipboard pressed to her chest. "I separated you because y'all talk too much, and you won't hear a word your guide says. You show me my best B.J., and we'll see about next time." She smiled like she and B.J. were old pals. "You can start by hiking yourself onto the seat before you break your neck."

As Ms. Quelling moved down the aisle, Chaperone Mom stepped into her place.

"Maybe you'll make some *new* friends today, B.J.," she said.

"I'll be your friend!" Kitty piped up.

B.J. glanced at her over her shoulder. "No offense or anything," she said. "But I already *have* friends."

Chaperone Mom gasped. "Now, that isn't nice!" She patted B.J. on the head and continued down the aisle.

"Busted," said Colton, wiggling his ears at B.J. Eddie let out a guffaw, and Colton punched him in the stomach.

"Boys are so lame," Maggie said. Her words placed themselves in a solid straight line, like fact blocks you couldn't possibly knock over. She looked at Sophie. "How come you hardly ever say anything?"

Sophie pulled her hood over her head, in spite of the Virginia-humid air. She wasn't sure when she could have squeezed a word into the conversation. Besides, she'd been too busy trying to figure out the possibilities.

For instance, *what did "B.J." stand for? Bambi Jo? Probably more like Bad Jerky.* B.J. looked as if she had just eaten some and was about to cough it back up.

And what about that Kitty person with the freckles? She must be Katherine, kept locked away in a tower, and she's so desperate to escape she clings to anyone she can reach. I'll save you! Rescue is my mission in life!

Antoinette tucked her long tresses beneath the hood of her dark cloak as she crept to the castle wall and gazed up at the tower.

"What are you looking at?"

Maggie's voice dropped on Sophie's daydream like a cement block. Sophie blinked at the bus ceiling above her.

"You think it's going to rain in here or what?" Maggie said. "I think you're a little strange."

"That's OK," Sophie said as she pushed back her hood. "Most people think I'm strange. My sister says I'm an alien from Planet Weird."

"Is that your real voice?" Maggie said.

Sophie didn't have a chance to tell her that, yes, the pipsqueak voice was the real thing, because the bus lurched forward and all its occupants squealed.

"Colonial Williamsburg, here we come!" Chaperone Mom shouted over the squeal-a-thon.

B.J. whirled again, her eyes fixed on the back of the bus like a jealous cat's.

Sophie turned to the window and curled her feet under her. As she watched the yellowing late September trees flip by in a blur, a heavy feeling fell over her head and shoulders, almost like a cloak — and *not* Antoinette's beautiful black velvet cape that shrouded her in soft mysterious folds from the dangers of the night.

This cloak felt like it was woven of sadness, and Sophie had been wearing it for six whole weeks, ever since her family had moved from Houston to the small town of Poquoson, Virginia.

Houston was a *huge* city with parks and museums and *big* libraries full of dream possibilities. Poquoson was mostly one street with a Farm Fresh grocery store and a Krispy Kreme Donut shop attached to a gas station, where hordes of mosquitoes flew through solid clouds of bug spray to gnaw on Sophie's legs.

The school was way different too. Here, Sophie had to change classes for every single subject, and that made it hard to keep up. It seemed as if she would just get settled into her seat in one class-room, when the bell sent her running to the next one, hauling her backpack, and leaving her work unfinished.

Of course, her new teachers had already told her — *and* her parents — that if she didn't stare out the window and daydream so much, she could get her work done before the end of class. In Houston the other students were used to her going off into daydreams. She hardly ever got teased about it there. But then her dad got promoted by NASA and moved the whole family to Virginia.

So the staring and taunting had started all over again since school started. This field trip was the first thing that even sounded like fun since they'd left Texas.

"Won't Williamsburg be amazing?" Sophie said to Maggie.

"No. Walking on the moon would be amazing. This is just historical."

Sophie sighed. "I wish it were French history. I want to learn about that. I'm into France."

Maggie pulled her chin in. "France? This is America."

"Is it?" Colton said. "Is it really? Hey, Eddie! This is America!"

"Huh?"

Colton gave him a left hook. "Maggot just said this is America. I thought we were in China, man."

"Don't call me maggot," Maggie said.

Sophie pulled her knees into a hug. Although her family hadn't had a chance to explore yet, Sophie's mother had collected brochures about the places they would go and had put Colonial Williamsburg at the top of the pile.

"They've restored one whole area just the way it was before and during the American Revolution," Mama had told her. "They say it's like stepping right back into the past."

"How long till we get there?" Sophie said. Maggie didn't answer. She whacked Colton with his own baseball cap, threw it at him, and then threatened both boys with their lives if they didn't stop calling her maggot.

"It isn't nice to hit boys," Chaperone Mom said. "It isn't nice to hit anybody."

"Why should I be nice to them?" Maggie said. "They sure aren't nice to me."

Sophie once again stared along the dense woods lining the highway and saw a sign appear, reading: Colonial Williamsburg. It had a little green shield on it, and Sophie felt a familiar flutter in her chest. This was real! It had its own little green shield and everything.

Sophie didn't hear Chaperone Mom's answer to Maggie. She geared up her imagination for an adventure — one that didn't include maggots or lame boys or anything not "nice" at all.

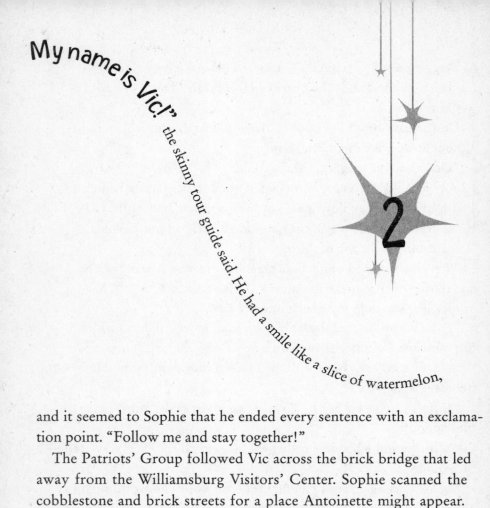

My name is Vic!" the skinny tour guide said. He had a smile like a slice of watermelon,

and it seemed to Sophie that he ended every sentence with an exclamation point. "Follow me and stay together!"

The Patriots' Group followed Vic across the brick bridge that led away from the Williamsburg Visitors' Center. Sophie scanned the cobblestone and brick streets for a place Antoinette might appear.

Maggie's foot smashed down the back of Sophie's sneaker. *I didn't think being field trip buddies meant we had to be Siamese twins,* Sophie thought. She picked up speed.

They passed along the side of a massive brick building with a curving wall and stopped in front of a tall iron gate. "This is the Governor's Palace," Vic informed them. "Several royal governors lived here, including Governor Alexander Spotswood—not a very nice character!"

Surely there's a place for Antoinette beyond these gates, Sophie thought. She squirmed through the Patriots to get a closer view. Those high walls held who-knew-*what* amazing secrets. But with Colton and Eddie howling and B.J. repeating "What?" over and over, Sophie couldn't even FIND Antoinette.

"We'll visit the Governor's Palace at the end of your tour!" Vic said. Sophie caught up to him and gave the palace a wistful, backward glance as they walked along, right in the middle of the street.

"Where are the cars?" she said.

Vic looked down at her with the same surprised expression most adults made when they heard her speak for the first time. "Young lady," he answered, "you will find the Duke of Gloucester Street precisely as you would have in the eighteenth century!"

I love that! Sophie thought. At that very moment, a carriage rumbled past, driven by a man wearing white stockings, a coat with tails, and a three-cornered hat. Sophie closed her eyes and listened to the *clip-clop* of the horses' hooves.

Antoinette LaCroix peeked from inside the carriage, her face half hidden by the hood of her cloak. All around her colonists hurried to and fro, calling to each other in English. She could understand them, but how she longed to hear her native French.

"Hey!"

Something smacked Sophie on the top of the head. She blinked at Maggie, who was holding her map rolled up like a billy club.

"Come on," Maggie said. "You're supposed to stay with the group." She dragged Sophie forward by the wrist to where the group stood on tiptoes at a cemetery wall.

"This is Bruton Parish Church!" Vic said. "We'll visit here on our way back, too!"

"Will we get to look at the graves?" Maggie said.

"Gross!" B.J. said. "Who wants to look at dead people?"

"Tombstones here date back to the 1600s!" Vic said, walking backward and beckoning the group with both hands. Sophie felt a delighted shiver.

Next they stopped in front of the courthouse. A man in a sweeping waistcoat and white silk stockings emerged through the tall wooden doors and shouted, "Nathaniel Buttonwick! Appear before the judge, or you will forfeit your recognizance!"

"What?" B.J. and Kitty said together.

Sophie didn't have any idea what *recognizance* meant either, but she loved the sound of it. Outside the courthouse two guards pushed a man's head through a hole in a wooden contraption and lowered a wooden railing over the man's wrists.

"In the stocks till sundown!" one guard shouted.

"He has to stand there until dark?" Sophie said.

"It's not real," Maggie said.

Antoinette was appalled. She had never seen such treatment, not in the gentle place from whence she came. Had it been a mistake to come to the colonies? But Antoinette shook her head until her tresses tossed against her face. She must find her mission.

Sophie wished she had a costume — like that little girl she saw across the street pushing a rolling hoop with a stick. She had on a white puffy cap and an apron-covered dress down to her ankles and white stockings that Sophie longed to feel on her own legs. A boy chased after her, trying to knock over her hoop.

I guess boys have always been annoying, Sophie thought. She caught up with Vic in time to hear that the powder magazine — an eight-sided brick building with a roof like a pointy hat — had once stored the cannons and guns and ammunition of Colonial Williamsburg's small army.

Sophie wanted to skip as they passed through an opening in the fence. A man with a big barrel chest suddenly blocked their path and bellowed, "Halt!"

"What?" B.J. and Kitty said.

"It's not real," Maggie said again, although she looked up at the giant of a man with reluctant respect in her eyes.

The man's tan shirt was the size of a pup tent, and the white scarf tied around his massive head framed a snarling face. Sophie swallowed hard.

"Fall in!" he shouted.

Colton fell to the ground, sending Eddie into a fit of boy-howls.

"That means fall into a straight line!"

The rest of them scrambled into place. The big man picked Colton up by his backpack and set him down on his feet next to Sophie.

"Hey, dude!" Colton said.

"You will call me Sergeant! Let me hear it!"

"Yes, Sergeant!" Sophie cried out.

Eddie went into convulsions of laughter. Colton said, "Yes, Sergeant," in a mousy voice.

"You — and you — fall out!" the sergeant roared.

Eddie and Colton were banished to a blue wagon full of long poles, where the sergeant told them to stay until further notice. When Chaperone Mom started to march over to them, the sergeant yelled, "You! Fall in!"

"Oh, no, I'm the chaperone!" she said.

"We need every able-bodied individual! We are no longer a small militia — we are part of the Colonial Army! If Lafayette and his troops do not arrive in time, it will be us against the Redcoats!"

Lafayette? Sophie thought. *That sounds like a French name.*

"Eyes left! Eyes front! Eyes left!" the sergeant commanded. When he said, "Pick up your arms!" the group scurried for the blue wagon and got their "guns" — long sticks almost twice as tall as Sophie. The sergeant told Eddie and Colton that he would give them one last chance, and they grabbed their sticks to line up with the rest.

"Left flank!" the sergeant cried, and he showed them how to stand their guns along their left legs. Then he taught them how to "load," how to shift from "flank" to "shoulder," how to "make ready" and "present" in one smooth motion, and to "make fire" only when he commanded. At those words, everyone screamed, "Boom!"

Antoinette had never held a weapon before in her life, but if this was what it took to fulfill her mission, then she could do it.

"Make ready!" the sergeant cried.

With her musket firmly in her hands, Antoinette dropped to her knee, waiting for the commands to present and fire.

"*You!* You there, soldier!"

Sophie looked into the sergeant's face and clung to her stick. "Yes, Sergeant?" she said.

"You're a fine soldier. You shame the whole lot of them. You can fight in my company any time."

"Thank you, Sergeant," Sophie said.

Afterward, Sophie floated happily down the street with the Patriots. She was now a part of Colonial Williamsburg — one of its finest soldiers.

"Hey, pipsqueak," Colton said to her.

Sophie glared at him. "That's *Corporal* Pipsqueak to you, *Private*."

"What's she talking about?" Eddie said.

"Nothing," Colton said. "She's whacked."

But right by Vic's elbow, with Maggie walking up her calves, Sophie felt anything but whacked as she made Williamsburg her own.

Inside the houses and shops, every detail swept her back across the centuries: a powdered wig on a dressing table, a quill pen in a china holder, and a four-poster bed with mosquito netting draped down its sides. *I want that in MY bedroom,* Sophie thought.

The formal English gardens with clipped hedges helped her picture Antoinette waiting among the flowers for the delivery of a secret message. And the little brick pathways covered in ivy leading down from the streets were custom-made for Antoinette's getaways.

She loved it *all*, including the sign above the jeweler's that said, "Engraving. Watch-Making. Done in the Beft Manner."

"Beft?" Sophie said.

Of course, B.J. said, "What?"

"Best," Maggie told her.

Sophie decided to start writing all of her S's that way from now on. She felt certain that Lafayette, whoever he was, had made his S's just like that.

When they stopped to have a picnic in the Market Square, Sophie inched close to Vic.

"Could you tell me about Lafayette?" she said.

"The Marquis de Lafayette was a young French nobleman," Vic said. "Red-headed, very short, and small-boned. He was only nineteen years old when he bought a ship and left France secretly to help the Colonists. Without him, the patriots might not have won the war, and we wouldn't be free today."

"He *bought* a whole ship?" Colton said. "He must've had cash."

"Lafayette used his wealth to help the American colonies because he believed in fairness," Vic said. "All his life he stood against anything that was more evil than good."

"So did he make it to Williamsburg in time?" Sophie said. "The sergeant said if he didn't get here with his troops, the militia would be on its own."

Vic gave her his big watermelon smile. "You were paying attention!"

"I was, too!" B.J. muttered to Kitty. They gave Sophie identical narrow-eyed stares.

"So did he get here in time?" Sophie said.

"He did! But there was almost disaster."

Sophie felt the flutter in her chest. Disaster always had possibilities.

"Lafayette moved his advance units to about ten miles north of here. Someone gave him false information — that most of the British Army had already crossed the James River. So he decided to move closer to Jamestown and attack whatever enemy troops remained."

"But the whole British Army was still there!" Sophie said.

"So did the Brits waste him?" Colton said.

"No," Vic said. "He learned about the trap and marched straight to Yorktown, where the war was won."

"Who told him about the trap?" Maggie said.

But Sophie didn't listen to the answer.

From her hiding place in the Market Square, Antoinette held her breath until the British Loyalists moved on. She didn't breathe from the time she heard their secret plans until she was sure they had gone into the Raleigh Tavern. Then she gathered up her skirts and ran for the carriage house. She had to reach the Marquis de Lafayette with the news — before he marched right into the British trap.

"Hey! Sophie!"

"*What?*" Sophie said.

She shook off the hand that Maggie had wrapped around her back-pack strap.

"Fine," Maggie said. Her eyes narrowed into fudge-colored slits. "I won't tell you that everybody else is going shopping." She put up her hands. "You're way too high-maintenance."

Faithgirlz Handbook,
Updated and Expanded

How to Let Your Faith Shine Through

Suzanne Hadley

Join the Best Club Around!

Discover the power true friendships can have! This handbook gives you all you need to become a Faithgirl and start your own incredible club of friends—a club where you share the secrets of life, real beauty, and what it really means to be BFFs. With fun games, giggle-inducing activities, and exciting devotions to share, your Faithgirlz club will be the place to be. Plus, as you grow closer to God together, you'll discover the amazing things he has in store for you. So grab your friends, old and new, and start a sisterhood like no other.

The Boarding School Mysteries
from Kristi Holl

The Boarding School Mysteries series challenges twelve-year-old Jeri McKane, a sixth grader at the private landmark School for Girls, to trust God's Word and direction as this amateur sleuth searches for clues in the midst of danger.

Vanished

Poisoned

Betrayed

Burned

Available in stores and online!

Faithgirlz! Devotions

What's a Girl to Do?

Finding Faith in Everyday Life

Kristi Holl

Ninety days of devotionals featuring everyday situations help girls take their faith walk from indifference to compassion, from critical to admiring, from anxious to peaceful, from worldly beauty to self-acceptance, and much more. Each story is paired with Scripture to help girls see the Bible does have answers.

Online with God

A 90-Day Devotional

Laurie Lazzaro Knowlton

Scripture verses, tips on making safe choices, and prayers for all the confusing times in your life. As you read it, you'll realize that God listens when you blog as well as when you pray. After all, he's the Lord of the universe—including cyberspace.

That Is SO Me: 365 Days of Devotions

Flip-Flops, Faith, and Friends

Nancy Rue

Take a daily step of faith. Here is the devotional you've been waiting for: a place for everyday inspiration for everyday girls. On your 365-day journey through the Bible, discover topics that will have you saying "That is SO me!" over and over and over again.

Available in stores and online!

Faithgirlz! Bibles

NIV Faithgirlz! Bible,
Revised Edition

Every girl wants to know she's totally unique and special. This Bible says that with Faithgirlz! sparkle! Now girls can grow closer to God as they discover the journey of a lifetime, in their language, for their world.

NIV Faithgirlz! Bible,
Revised Edition

Same great Bible, way cool cover.

Italian Duo-Tone™, Spring Green/Petal Purple

NIV Faithgirlz! Backpack Bible,
Revised Edition

Small enough to fit into a backpack or bag, this Bible can go anywhere. With an Italian Duo-Tone™ pink design, features include twelve full-color pages of Faithgirlz fun that helps girls learn the "Beauty of Believing!"

Italian Duo-Tone™, Pink

Available in stores and online!

We want to hear from you. Please send your comments about this book to us in care of zreview@zondervan.com. Thank you.

ZONDERVAN.com/
AUTHORTRACKER
follow your favorite authors